FREE MAREE

When Faith, Family, and Freedom Collide

Maree P. Gauper

Cover designed by R.J. Gauper
Illustrations by Maree P. Gauper

Although the main events described in this book took place 35 years ago, all the major facts are true to the best of my knowledge. I have written my story based on my notes, diary entries and memories of the period. Chapters composed in the third person describe events in which I was obviously not present, since I was being held elsewhere. In the spirit of creative non-fiction, I did my best to re-create scenes and dialog that might well have happened, based on interviews with those who were present and newspaper reports from that time. Some names have been changed for individuals who still fear that their jobs or livelihoods might be threatened if their religious affiliations were to be publicly known.

Maree P. Gauper
Visit my website: freemaree.com

Printed in the United States of America

First Printing: Jan 2019
Free Maree

ISBN-978-1-7335862-0-7

CONTENTS

To Toru Goto,
who was confined for over
twelve years, and to all
deprogramming survivors.

(See appendix 2)

FOREWORD

Free Maree goes way beyond the typical coming of age story. This memoir has it all, starting with family conflict centered on Maree's unusual choice of faith. There's betrayal, mystery, anxiety and grief. It's an exploration of values and what love and friendship is really about. It's about keeping hope alive when there's nothing but a bare cell-like room and the empty company of strangers. And it's a long-distance love story with a commitment to purity that's rarely seen in this hedonistic age.

Set in New Zealand, with brief trips to Australia and New York City, the reader will be taken into another culture and a different worldview. *Free Maree* dives deep into a typical working class Irish Catholic family living at the southern tip of the islands of New Zealand.

The matriarch of the Ryan family and her large brood are appalled at the life Maree has found, and delights in. Her family is at odds with a spiritual commitment they don't know and cannot fathom. How could Maree be captivated by the Reverend Sun Myung Moon's Unification Church? It's unthinkable! She must be brainwashed! That's the only possibility.

As a Christian and a psychotherapist, I often discuss the vital issue of free will with my clients. God gives us the ability to freely make choices—for good or ill. This issue of free will becomes a serious problem when those, with either evil or simply hurtful intent, attempt to force their will upon another.

Enter the deprogrammers.

Memoirs give the reader a chance to live vicariously for a few hours or days. A fresh look at life is guaranteed by this true-life drama.

Free Maree is a page-turner. Get at it.

Susan Perkins McNally, Ph.D., LMFT, Yuba City, CA

Dr. McNally

PROLOGUE

A man's foes will be those from his own household.
—Matthew 10:36

During the 1970s, new religious groups seemed to be everywhere. The Children of God, Hare Krishna, Scientology and others grew rapidly in America and around the world, attracting thousands of converts in their late teens or early twenties. Young people of that era, being famously disillusioned with the "establishment," saw in these new groups a way to fill a certain void in their lives. Many found solace, hope and new direction.

Sensational press coverage, often overtly hostile to the new religions, fueled widespread concern. Some alarmed parents became activists against the new religions, joining forces with clergy, mental health professionals and self-proclaimed cult experts. The Anti-Cult Movement (ACM) was born.

From the ACM's viewpoint, large numbers of young adults were joining weird new groups, abandoning the faith of their parents, even dropping out of school; this meant that these kids were being brainwashed, and something needed to be done.

Enter the deprogrammers, wannabe knights in shining armor able to rescue children who had allegedly been subject to mind control. They could make them snap out of it. All they needed was a few days with the victim to successfully reverse the effects of so-called brainwashing. On the downside, they would have to physically abduct the subject. They also charged outrageous fees for these services despite the fact that they typically had no mental health credentials whatsoever.

In 1977 at the age of 19, I became a member of a new religious movement. After several unsuccessful attempts to remove me from my new religion, my devout Catholic parents hired an American deprogramming team in August of 1983.

This is an account of the events surrounding my sudden disappearance, which generated nationwide media attention in my native New Zealand at that time.

Dr Mose Durst writes in his book, *To Bigotry, No Sanction,* "... the public believes that when deprogramming occurs, it is only in the context of cults, and thus is to be tolerated. The real story of this violent abuse of religious liberty is yet to be told."

I hope that my story will help set the record straight.

GLOSSARY OF TERMS

Arsehole: asshole. A despicable person.
Australia: a large island to the northwest of New Zealand*.
Bach: (pronounced *batch*) a vacation home (North Island of New Zealand).
Bollocks: a cry to express disbelief, similar to "bullshit" in American usage; literally, testicles.
Brassed off: pissed off, annoyed, vexed.
Brownie points: an imaginary award given to someone who does good deeds.
Crayfish: New Zealand rock lobster.
Flat: Apartment.
Helen Caldicott: Australian physician, author and anti-nuclear activist.
Kiwi: iconic flightless bird native to New Zealand; a New Zealand person.
Mansei: a Korean expression meaning "victory for 10,000 years," roughly equivalent to "Hooray!"
Milo: a malted, chocolate-flavored drink mix.
Motorway: freeway.
Shout: treat.
Solicitor: in British English, a member of the legal profession.
Thin edge of the wedge: tip of the iceberg.
Vegemite: a savory spread made from leftover brewers' yeast extract.

Waitemata City: a city in the greater Auckland area, formed in 1974, later reorganized to become the modern city of Waitakere.
Weetabix, Weet-Bix: a high fiber, low-sugar breakfast cereal biscuit manufactured in Australia and New Zealand by the Sanitarium Health Company.
Won't be a tick: won't be a second.
Zealandia: New Zealand tabloid newspaper published weekly by the Catholic Bishop of Auckland until 1989.

*Just kidding. It's a country and continent, geographically and politically separate from its close neighbor, New Zealand.

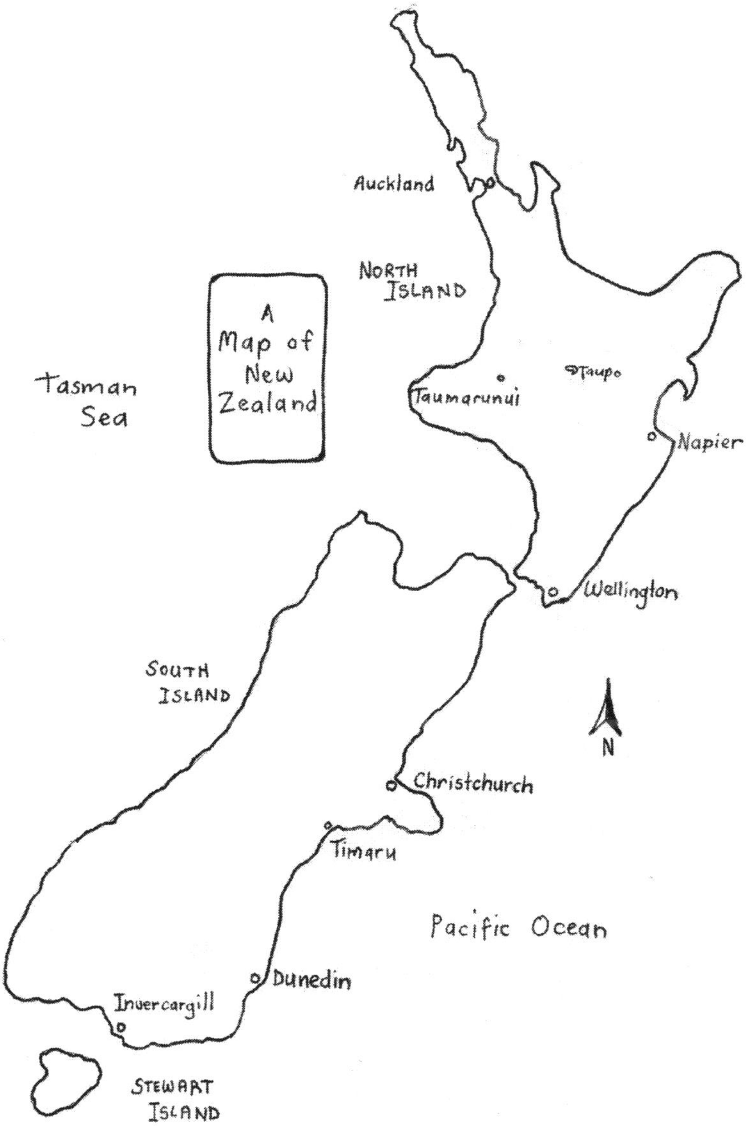
Auckland
NORTH ISLAND
A Map of New Zealand
Tasman Sea
Taumarunui
Taupo
Napier
Wellington
SOUTH ISLAND
N
Christchurch
Timaru
Pacific Ocean
Dunedin
Invercargill
STEWART ISLAND

Map Showing City of Auckland
N.Z. and greater Auckland area.
Kidnappers' hideout
Army Bay
Whangaparaoa Peninsula
N
Silverdale
Torbay
Browns Bay
Campbells Bay
Castor Bay
Albany
Takapuna
Devonport
Te Atatu Peninsula
Waitemata Harbor
Downtown Auckland
Herne Bay Peninsula
Waitemata
(Waitakere)
Parnell
Mt Albert
Epsom

1 – "ET TU, BRUTE?"

Et tu, Brute?
— **William Shakespeare, Julius Caesar**

Caesar utters this Latin phrase meaning:
***Even you, Brutus?* in Act III Scene 1 as he is being stabbed to death,**
having recognized his friend Brutus as one of the assassins.

1983, New Zealand

Something weird was going on. We should have been heading out to the suburbs where David lived, so why was Paul suddenly turning right, into a dead-end alley? And stopping the car?

Several startling things happened all at once: two strange men opened the back doors of the car and got in on either side of me; and Celine got out.

What's happening? What's going on?

A few days earlier

One of the best things about being back in Auckland was getting in touch with old friends like Celine. In April, when I'd called her for the first time, she'd hopped on her bicycle and come over to see me, all the way from Ponsonby, within half an hour of my phone call. I was overjoyed to see her again and from then on, we tried to get together on a regular basis.

I was thrilled the night she invited me to dinner.

"Paul and David want us to get together for a reunion," she explained over the phone.

"That sounds great, just like old times. It's ages since the last time I saw David."

"Yes. We'll have a lot of catching up to do."

"That's for sure. I wonder if we should make a point of NOT discussing politics?"

Celine laughed, remembering an earlier conversation between the two of us, about Ronald Reagan and the CIA, that had become quite heated.

"Good idea. Then we're to rendezvous with Paul downtown at 5 o'clock Thursday, and he'll drive us to David's. Where's a good place for you and I to meet?"

"Um, how about the corner of Queen Street and Victoria?" The intersection would be a quick walk from our witnessing center.

"Sounds perfect. I'll see you then!"

I hung up the telephone receiver and looked forward to the get together.

Sweet, kind, beautiful Celine had been one of my best friends when I was a student at the university in Dunedin in the 1970s. A rock of support during the dark days when my atheist flat-mates tormented me for my Catholic faith, she'd also been a loyal cheerleader through my weight loss journey, having waged a similar battle herself. Paul and David played similar but more minor roles.

Back then, we were both devout Catholic girls who saw eye-to-eye on almost everything. Now, we found ourselves on different spiritual paths and opposite sides of the political spectrum, yet the friendship endured. Or so I thought.

It was 1983. Ronald Reagan was President of the United States and Yuri Andropov was a dark lord in charge of an Evil Empire, if you were to believe Reagan, which I did. *Return of the Jedi*, the third of the *Star Wars* movies, was released that year. In *Star Wars* and in real life, it seemed, there was a fierce battle between good and evil.

The Cold War was heating up between the U.S. and its Communist enemies, accompanied by an alarming buildup of nuclear weapons on both sides. Celine was active in New Zealand's growing anti-nuclear movement. She attended Helen Caldicott rallies, wore tee-shirts with political slogans and wrote articles for the *Zealandia*.

By August, I'd been in Auckland about five months, staying in the Unification Church center in Parnell, having been assigned as assistant to the National Leader. I lived with a community of about 20 full-time lay missionaries whose goal was to achieve world peace through the unification of religions.

Most days, we went out to raise funds to support our small community, selling framed prints and other inexpensive items door-to-door. Otherwise, we walked the streets of the city, approaching passers-by to engage them in conversation and share with them about our new movement and its vision. This witnessing was our standard way of winning new members. It was how most of us had been introduced to the church.

Witnessing was tough in Auckland. I'd enjoyed it in Australia and even had some success. In Auckland, no one seemed to want to stop and talk. They seemed to be annoyed or in a hurry. Possibly we had been overly zealous in the past and people were tired of us.

Since it was hard dealing with rejection day after day, I was doubly glad to get the invitation from Celine. It would be a welcome break from my daily routine.

Thursday, August 4, 1983.

It had been a good day so far. A nice woman I met while street witnessing told me I looked like the actress, Meryl Streep. Being a big fan of Meryl I was flattered by the comparison and it gave my confidence a needed boost.

Above the normal buzz of the busy city, someone was playing *Karma Chameleon.* I mindlessly sang along with Boy George as I walked down the sloping sidewalk of Victoria Street, zipping up my white woolen sweater against the chilly air. I pushed back a thick sleeve enough to check the time on my watch. It was a few minutes before five. *Good, I'll be on time*. I smiled as I thought about the watch and the special young man who had given it to me. Above me sat the Auckland domain, the university and hospital. Downhill were the shops and office buildings of Queen Street. From my vantage point I could see Celine before she saw me.

Celine's long blonde hair had a couple of spiraling strands which curled down in front of her ears in feathery corkscrews. They made me think of my old principal, Sister Marie Therese, who had forbidden such frivolities at our high school for Catholic girls. I could still hear her voice:

"These *doodles* are not permitted with your school uniform!"

Thank goodness those days were over.

Celine had always been nervous. Besides her slight stutter, another sign of anxiety was her habit of twisting those long curly strands around an index finger.

Which is exactly what she was doing that evening of August 4. While I was relaxed and ready for a happy reunion of old friends,

Celine was sitting on a low concrete bench on the street corner, tugging and twirling a corkscrew curl.

What's wrong, Celine?

Something wasn't right, and deep inside me an alarm was sounding, but I chose to ignore it.

We exchanged small talk for a while, but it felt strained, which only increased my suspicion that Celine was anxious about something.

Perhaps she's not feeling well? Before I had a chance to ask, Paul's car appeared and pulled up to the curb along Queen Street, skillfully navigating the rush-hour traffic. It was about five o'clock. Celine got into the front passenger seat and I climbed into the back.

It was great to see Paul. He was a sweetheart. We'd gone to the same primary school in my hometown of Invercargill, so I'd known him most of my life. He was tall and angular, not especially handsome, but funny and good-natured. He'd once bought me a bottle of *Charlie* perfume just because I liked it.

By 1983 Paul was a pharmacist in Auckland. One day, while fundraising in the northern suburb of Albany, I happened to walk into his pharmacy. He cheerfully bought several of whatever I was selling, and I was grateful that an old friend would be so kind and supportive. Not long after that, he invited me up to his place for dinner, and I went, accompanied by a church brother as I didn't drive at that time. We had an enjoyable evening with Paul and the couple that lived with him.

Right now, something weird was going on. We should have been heading out to the suburbs where David lived, so why was Paul suddenly turning right, into a dead-end alley, and stopping the car?

Several startling things happened all at once: two strange men opened the back doors of the car and got in on either side of me; and Celine *got out.* I felt my body tense and my heart rate started speeding.

Why is she getting out? Who are these people?

An older woman with gray hair tied in a head scarf got into the front passenger seat. Three doors had just opened and all three quickly slammed shut, then we were moving again, back into the heavy traffic.

What's happening? What's going on?

While I was still struggling to comprehend the frightening turn of events, the strange woman in the front seat turned around, removing her head scarf *and her hair*, or so it seemed, as the gray curls came off along with the scarf.

It was a wig, a disguise to hide the woman's identity, now plain to see as she turned around to face me. My mother said, "Maree, we're doing this for your own good."

Nooooooooo!

I should have seen this coming, but I hadn't.

Inwardly groaning with dismay and apprehension, I sank down into the seat. The moment I recognized my mother, I knew exactly what was going on. They were going to try and "deprogram" me. There would be no dinner at David's that night. I'd been set up by my so-called friends.

Paralyzed with fright, I had no idea what to do. I felt my heart racing and a thumping pulse in my eardrums. Wedged between two strong-looking young men, I just sat there, frozen, as waves of emotion swept over me.

I was a twenty-five-year-old woman being kidnapped by my own mother.

2 - SEA OF BITTERNESS

The Irish family, like the Jewish one, is noted for its dominant maternal figure, who tries to keep control of her children long after they have outgrown their teen years.

—Felix Donnelly, *One Priest's Life*

1990

One night I had a vivid dream in which I was walking with my mother. She was talking to me and her words were angry, scornful, critical and accusing. Suddenly, instead of words, vomit began to come out of her mouth until she had vomited all over herself, becoming so revolting that I recoiled in horror; and as she fell to the ground in a disgusting heap, I turned to look for a phone booth so that somebody – anyone but me – would have to deal with this stinking mess.

As I was lifting the telephone receiver, a stranger approached. He had a beard and wore a long white robe and looked like Jesus. I watched him bend over and pick up my filthy mother, kindly and gently as if she were a small child that he was cradling in his arms.

Holding her, he looked directly at me. Instead of smiling kindly like I wanted him to, he was serious and stern. The look that he gave me said something like, "If I can forgive her, so can you."

* * *

It wasn't that Mum was a bad person. She had been an exemplary mother, utterly devoted to her family and as hard-working as a parent could be. During my childhood she was a fulltime housewife and mother of seven, who sewed, knitted, washed, dried, ironed, mended and altered. She cooked, baked, preserved, composted, gardened and cleaned.

We lived in Invercargill, a small city at the bottom of the world, and one of the most miserable on a frosty winter morning. Yet, for most of the 1960s when we had a coal range, it was Mum who got up before everyone, to light the coal fire for heat and cooking, beneath a picture of the Sacred Heart of Jesus.

It was a time when men didn't help around the house. Dad also worked hard, as a builder, lifting heavy wet lumber day after day. Once dinner was over, he settled into his armchair and didn't move until bedtime.

Mum seemed to enjoy taking care of her family, except when we broke things or got into fights (which seemed to happen a lot) or when she didn't feel well.

I recollect one night when I was 8 or 9, and we were sitting in the living room watching TV. Dad was in his special chair, the rest of us wherever we could claim a spot on the sofa, except for Mum, who was kneeling on the floor, changing the diaper of whoever was the baby at the time. Her eyes were red, and I saw clear liquid dripping from her nose.

"Mummy, why are you crying?"

"Because I'm sick, that's why."

I cringed at the sharp response, but also felt bad that she was still working even though she was sick.

I didn't know how to change a baby. I'd tried, but it was hard to get safety-pins through the thick layers of cotton and flannel. You could easily prick yourself with the pin, or worse, you could prick the baby. I wished Dad would do something, but I don't think he knew how to change a diaper either. He just kept sitting.

Education was a serious matter. Mum helped us with our homework if necessary. When I once had trouble remembering that two pints equaled one quart, Mum went to the pantry, brought out two pint-bottles of milk and held them up.

"Look! Two pints equal one quart!" then somehow the slick glass containers slipped out of her grasp and smashed near the hearth in front of the coal range. The Sacred Heart of Jesus looked on, unperturbed, as Mum knelt to clean up the mess. She looked up at me with an angry face, even though it wasn't my fault.

"Now you'll *never* forget it."

We were about as Catholic as it was possible to be, as were our friends, relations and Irish ancestors all the way back to the time of St Patrick.

There were also non-Catholics in my small world; some lived in our own neighborhood. They were nice people, but *we* were going to heaven, and they were not. One time I asked my mother why we didn't warn those neighbors that they were on the wrong track. Mum was in the pantry on her kitchen stool, peeling potatoes, which she did every night.

"That would be embarrassing," said Mum quickly, without looking up from the potatoes.

In my childish mind I didn't question her wisdom, even though it implied that anything, even eternal hell-fire, was preferable to embarrassment.

***

Mum was slender and blue-eyed. Her name was Mary. Catholics had a long tradition of naming at least one of their children Mary out of devotion to the Blessed Virgin. Consequently, it became the most popular girl's name in the Christian world.

My father's only sister was a Mary. Dad's twin brothers each married a Mary just as Dad had, so I had three Auntie Marys and my Uncle Kevin's kids had four, my mother being one of them.

To save confusion, Mum would hyphenate each Mary's name with the name of her husband, so that a telephone conversation might go something like, "Hello, Mary-Ray? This is Mary-Paul. I was just talking with Mary-Mick about having a get-together at Mary-Pat's for Easter Sunday..."

Perhaps because of the multitude of Marys, I was named Maree, an English spelling of "Marie," the French version of Mary. Like a lot of Australians and New Zealanders, we spelled my name with the double *e* and no *i* which many years later would confuse the heck out of Americans. I used to tell people that my father didn't know how to spell when he filled in my birth certificate.

The name and its variations mean "sea of bitterness." Was that a bad omen? Growing up, I never imagined there would someday be bitterness between me and my mother.

I was a well-behaved child. I took piano and violin lessons and played in the local youth orchestra. I did well in school and was usually near the top of my class. Mum and I had a pretty good relationship for most of my life; at least, until I decided to change my religion. That was the beginning of the bitterness.

Religion, which bound our family together, was also what pulled us apart.

At age 19, after I joined the Unification Church, my family told me I was in a dangerous cult. *Time* and *Newsweek* had recently revealed sensational details of the 'cult phenomenon.' My parents trusted *Time* and *Newsweek* more than they trusted me.

They went immediately into rescue mode. Over the next few years, my mother compiled mountains of "anti-cult" material, condensing it into a continuing stream of hate mail. She became a modern-day Inquisitor.

The letters were always in her distinctive, spidery cursive:

Maree,

These cults are all the same. The Children of God, Hare Krishna, Moonists and other weird groups, they all use the same techniques to control and manipulate their new recruits. Long hours of indoctrination, low-protein diet, sleep deprivation, separation from their families. They're the same techniques used by the communists to brainwash their prisoners-of-war.

Moon is not the messiah, he's a millionaire industrialist using young people like you to enrich himself and his family. He lives in a mansion and drives a Lincoln Continental, while his minions (like you) go out begging on the streets. It's not right. I hope and pray you will soon understand that.

Your loving,

Mum.

That evening, when she removed her disguise, I recognized her, not only as my mother, but as my enemy.

3 - COUNTRY ROADS

Kidnapping causes a long-term rupture in the psyche of those kidnapped and of those who wait for their return.
—Uzodinma Iweala

Shock and disbelief soon gave way to the bitter realization of having been deceived and betrayed by my friends and family. Then came the litanies of self-accusation for my own stupidity.

How could they? I trusted them. How long were they conspiring against me? Was all their friendliness nothing but a charade? I knew my family might try something like this, but I hadn't imagined their tentacles would reach all the way to my friends who lived in Auckland. Why hadn't I been more vigilant? I let myself be handed over to the enemy by two Judases. How could I have been so blind?

In 1977, Mum had shown up unannounced at the Melbourne Church center with my sister and a policeman, saying that I had stolen her Brownie Box camera. Mum lent me the camera when I left for Australia. I had to go to the police station to be interviewed. Once there, no one was interested in the camera. They were all trying to convince me to see a hypnotherapist from Tasmania.

I still remembered the scene vividly. Kurt, a tall thin church brother, had followed us to the station in the church center's little white car. He was there watching when I initially said yes to the idea of a hypnotherapist. I was 19 years old and naïve; it sounded harmless and maybe even fun, but Kurt was alarmed.

"No, don't go! This is just a trick."

The seriousness in his voice made me stop and sense the danger lurking behind the invitation. My sister, Christine, pulled me by my right hand.

"You have to come with us!"

Kurt took my left hand.

"No, Maree, don't listen to them!"

I was in the middle of a human tug-of-war. I chose Kurt and went back to the center in the white car, shaken by the ordeal, and thankful to Kurt for saving me.

The Tasmanian hypnotherapist turned out to be a known deprogrammer. That was Mum's first try.

In 1981 the same sister visited me again, in Sydney. We had a lovely picnic lunch with bread, French cheeses and some baklava, on a hill overlooking the famous Opera House that was shaped like the wedges of an orange. While we ate, she said I should come home for Christmas. She kept insisting and I felt uncomfortable.

Around the same time, I got a letter from my other sister, Anne, pleading with me to come home for Christmas. Certain things she wrote struck fear into me.

"...you needn't worry, there will be no deprogrammers...anyway, there's no deprogrammers in New Zealand and it costs thousands to get them out here..."

The more they begged, the less I wanted to go. *They were up to something.*

They were still up to something. That never stopped, and I foolishly stepped into their trap. How had I not known?

We were on our way out of the Auckland business district, approaching the northern motorway. Paul kept his eyes on the road, saying nothing. Jerking her head in Paul's direction while glancing back at me, my mother said,

"This man is one of your best friends in the whole world."

I glared at Paul, who looked uncomfortable.

Sure, Mum. Just what every girl needs, a two-faced, back-stabbing traitor to keep her on her toes.

My next impulse was to flee.

Here I was in a car, with my mother, two complete strangers and my "best friend in the whole world," on our way to an unknown destination.

I'd heard of kidnap victims being taken *legally* by their families because they could get a thing called a conservatorship from a judge.

What if they did that to me? What if they determined I was mentally ill and had me committed?

I needed to get away from these people, but how?

As we ascended over the Auckland Harbor Bridge in the thick of rush-hour traffic, I wondered if I should lurch forward, grab the steering wheel and make the car crash.

Maybe the police would come, and I could escape.

What if I cause some innocent person to be hurt or killed? The harbor bridge had eight lanes and was over a mile long. Every year there were dozens of accidents, some with serious injuries and fatalities. It was dangerous even to change lanes.

I decided against that wild stunt. Beside the danger, it might look like I *was* crazy. Any attempt to physically escape from this situation would probably be a waste of time. I was outnumbered four to one, and I was not strong, fast or athletic.

My best weapon would have to be my mind. *Concentrate. Think clearly.*

I tried to notice everything. There was a strange man on either side of me. Both stared out their side windows, avoiding eye contact and making no attempt at conversation. One was short and stocky while the other sat taller and had a lighter build.

As we drove further north, the taller guy started singing the John Denver song, *Take Me Home, Country Roads*, which struck me as ridiculous and unbelievably incongruous.

What an idiot!

Did these guys always sing John Denver songs while they abducted people? How surreal. I still hate that song.

The sprawling City of Auckland was beginning to thin out. My mind drifted. I began to remember a terrifying nightmare from years ago.

My mother and sister were visiting me in Australia...they looked so evil, I treated them with disdain...Mum had made an appointment for me to see a hypnotherapist who was a deprogrammer...I had to shake hands with him...he was a small Asian, a midget with a smiling face, but his hands were deformed...he made me shake his left hand as well as his right...it was repulsive...I wanted someone to help me but no one seemed aware...then I was walking across a bridge toward the deprogrammer when suddenly the bridge sloped down into the water, and I called out, "Jesus!"

I had the dream around the time my sisters were begging me to go home for Christmas, and its warning was clear. I would not go home, it wasn't safe. I shuddered at the memory, my teeth chattering.

We'd been traveling north for about an hour. The landscape was becoming green and sparsely populated. I noticed signs welcoming us to the Hibiscus Coast.

Then we turned right.

We had entered the Whangaparaoa peninsula, a resort area with beautiful beaches. The name means "Bay of Whales" in the Maori language. There are pods of orca and dolphin in the local waters. At the time, I had no idea where I was, and whale-watching wasn't on my mind. I continued to concentrate as hard as I could.

Silently we kept traveling east, down a long road. In the fading light, I could see houses on the right and beaches on the left.

When we finally stopped outside a house, it was dark.

Later I would learn that a middle-aged couple owned this beach house, which they made available for "deprogramming" sessions of Unification Church members. They were part of an organized local network of activist parents.

Should I make a run for it?

Before I had time to decide, the two strange men grabbed me firmly by each elbow and escorted me into the building, a modest one-storied vacation home. Passing through the main living area, I noticed a kitchen and dining area to my right, a TV set and sofas to my left. The men led me down a short hallway into a drab little room with a single bed and little else besides a chair.

This would be my cell.

I could hardly believe this was happening. My head was spinning with questions.

What will they do to me? Can I get away? How long will I have to stay here? Why did this happen to me? What will my friends, my real *friends, back at the church think when I don't come back?* They would be frantic. I needed to call them.

"Could I make a phone call?" I asked the men. "My friends will be worried."

"No. No phone calls," the short man growled.

I sat on the bed, shaken and numb, trying to steady myself for the battle I knew was about to begin.

4 - PRISONS DARK

They took my joy,
sifted it under a microscopic eye
and called God a chemical in my cell
and offered to remove it
so I could live normally.
—Ramona Josh

I was still sitting on the edge of the bed when a tall, lean, stoop-shouldered stranger walked in. He was over six feet tall and probably in his 30s, with short dark hair and a black horseshoe moustache. He wore a plaid shirt and blue jeans like a cowboy without a hat. As soon as he spoke, I knew he was American.

"We're here to help you think for yourself," he announced gruffly, throwing back his shoulders and towering over me, his tone condescending and belligerent.

Too bad, I already do that!

"We're here to help you free your mind. You'll get to look at material about the Unification Church that you wouldn't otherwise have access to. You're so controlled by the group you don't even know how to think for yourself."

Yes, I do!

"You're unquestioningly obedient, a willing slave. Think about it. When was the last time you made an independent decision, an independent judgement?"

How about the dumb decision to go out with my friends tonight?

Usually I liked people and found them interesting. Not this guy. He seemed to have already determined that I was his enemy and therefore he hated me.

How do you hate someone you don't even know?

"You're controlled by Moon and his underlings. It's a totalist movement."

Is not. How would you know, anyway? I'd never heard the term *totalist* before. I assumed he meant *totalitarian*.

For someone meeting me for the first time, Mr. Cowboy sure thought he knew a lot about me. As he continued to lecture, I wondered who *he* was, since he hadn't bothered to say.

I knew he was a practitioner of so-called deprogramming. We church members preferred the term "faith-breaking." Deprogramming, as a term, was demeaning since it implied we were programmed in the first place. In reality, these people would attempt to take a person's faith and rip it to shreds. They were the faith-breakers. My friend Mike Treacy had survived a faith-breaking experience a few years ago in Australia, and I learned a lot from his testimony. Like most Unification Church members, I had heard the fearful name Ted Patrick, pioneer of this despicable practice. I had a vague idea that Patrick was supposed to be in jail.

Earlier in 1983 there had been a spate of faith-breakings in New Zealand which generated some publicity. New Zealanders who joined the movement overseas came home to see their families; while doing so they were abducted by professional faith-breakers and ended up leaving the church.

Their public statements to the press followed a predictable formula.

"I was young and vulnerable when I unknowingly became involved in a dangerous cult and got brainwashed by them. Thanks to my parents and these wonderful deprogrammers, I'm now a free-thinking person again."

Because of such cases, we suspected that American faith-breakers might be operating in New Zealand. My friend Chris Newman made a point of keeping up with the latest developments in matters of religious freedom. I remembered him mentioning the name Joe Alexander with regard to the American faith-breaking phenomenon. He'd dismissively called Alexander a "used car salesman" who'd finally been convicted of his crimes and was now on probation.

Could this be Joe Alexander?

"You think Moon is the messiah." The cowboy was mocking me, his accent grating on my nerves. "If he's really the messiah, why does he need bodyguards? Can't God protect him?"

I don't know! Maybe God works through bodyguards, ever think of that?

"Why do you have to peddle stuff and make money for him? Doesn't he have enough already?"

It's not for him, you moron, it's for our own community.

For a year I had been a bookkeeper at the Melbourne church and I knew exactly where the money went.

"They're just manipulating you. You go out peddling and recruiting and get brownie points from Mr. Moon. You think your parents are Satan and everyone else is Satan except you and your fellow Moonies."

Oh my God. I don't think everyone's Satan, but you're getting close, Mister.

"You don't question anything because doubting and questioning is Satanic..."

Oh, really? There were several questions on my mind right at that moment.

Who is this person, and will he ever take a breath, so I can tell him how wrong he is about everything? Do they serve food in this place? (It was long past dinnertime and my stomach was growling.) *And what's a brownie point?*

"Dinner's ready, Joe," a voice called out, from beyond the bedroom.

I felt my eyes widen and my heart beat faster as I heard the name.

Joe. This must be the infamous Joe Alexander.

Joe answered the call and left the room just as a woman entered, delivering a plate of food for me. Dinner was tasty, probably home cooked and there were home baked cookies for dessert. Who was making this stuff? I imagined clueless helpful people delivering baked goods and casseroles to the house, like they do after a death in the family or when someone has a terminal illness. I wished I could find them and shout at them.

"What are you doing? This is not a wake, it's a kidnapping!"

The woman who brought the food was about my age, with straight, shoulder-length dark hair. She was dressed completely in black. When she introduced herself as Mary, I recognized her as one of the recently deprogrammed women from the newspaper stories.

As I ate, Mary politely explained to me in a flat sort of monotone, some of the rules:

"I'll be sleeping on the floor of your room. Windows are all boarded up, so you can't escape through them. There will be someone outside your door through the night. Light-bulbs will be removed overnight from lamps. As you can see, the ceiling bulb is already gone. Some deprogrammees become violent; one smashed a lightbulb and used the broken pieces to slice open her wrists. She had to be hospitalized and then escaped. You will use paper or Styrofoam plates and plastic utensils, because dishware or silverware can be used as weapons to harm yourself or others. I will accompany you to the bathroom whenever you need to go."

It was a lot to take in. They needn't have bothered with the precautions. I wasn't a suicide risk and I wasn't about to fight my way out of there. The odds would be against me by a long shot.

The bathroom rule was disconcerting. So, I couldn't even make a bowel movement with privacy? How unpleasant. It was hard to feel resentment toward Mary, however. There was something sad and empty about her. I felt sorry for her.

I was still finishing dinner with my plastic fork when Cowboy Joe swaggered back in. Taking control, he immediately got back to business. As before, he stood over me, thumbs in his jean pockets, occasionally moving one hand to stroke his dark moustache. He rarely made eye contact, as though performing a rehearsed soliloquy. His arrogant attitude was obnoxious.

"We're here to free your mind. The truth will set you free."

I don't need freeing.

"What do you call Moon? Father? The Bible says you should call no one your father on earth for you have one Father who is in heaven."

I called Catholic priests "Father" my whole life, you moron. What are you, some theology expert?

"You've been brainwashed by Moon and his people. You gave up your autonomy and you mindlessly follow orders."

I do not!

"They use fear and guilt to manipulate and control you. They use psychology and brainwashing techniques like the Chinese and North Korean communists used on their prisoners. It's mind control."

Just as my mother's been telling me for years and years.

He showed me a business card that read "Mose Durst, PhD." Dr Durst was a beloved and exemplary church leader in the San Francisco Bay Area. Many young people joined the movement under his leadership, including Australians and New Zealanders. "Mose Durst doesn't have a PhD," growled Joe. "He's a fraud. Kristina, his underling, majored in Psychology. That's how they developed the mind control techniques that are used in the Oakland church. They close your mind to everything but their absolute ideas. It's thought reform, brainwashing."

Your opinion, not mine.

His voice grew louder and more commanding, as though building to a climactic point in his prepared speech.

"God gave you a mind to think with. Use it! Think for yourself. Moon is no messiah. What he is, is a pimp, and you're nothing but a prostitute. You've given yourself to him body and soul. You're not out there selling flowers and candy, you're selling yourself and giving the money to that pimp."

What's a pimp?

"I don't care how long it takes. I just want you to think for yourself. We can stay here three, four months or longer. However long it takes."

Three or four months? What a frightening thought. I had a tentative plan in mind which involved a prepared breakdown on the third day, Mike Treacy style. If I could pull that off, would they let me go? Or would they send me to that rehabilitation place I'd heard about in Tucson, Arizona? What if I couldn't pull it off?

Joe finally ran out of gas at about 10:00 pm and left the room.

Thank God.

It had been an intense evening and I was feeling shaken, in need of solace. I could hardly believe this was really happening. I also couldn't believe I'd been stupid enough to fall for the trick my old friends had played, pretending to invite me out for dinner. I should have suspected something; I was too trusting. The pain of betrayal was fresh. It stung. *How could they do that to me?*

I needed to center myself. Reading something spiritual was usually helpful, but if I asked for a *Divine Principle* (a textbook of the teachings of the Unification Church), that would no doubt be against their rules. I took a chance and asked for a Bible. Luckily, that was acceptable, and someone brought one in for me. They seemed pleased that I had asked.

As I got ready for bed Mary shadowed my every move. She was a slightly built woman with a fair complexion. With the right colors and a little animation, she might have been attractive. She didn't say much, but after listening to Joe all evening it was a relief to be with someone quiet. Just before she took out the last light bulb, I had enough time to pray quickly and open the Bible.

Oh God, I'm sorry this is happening. I wish it wasn't happening! Please help me! Why am I here and how can I get through it?

I shut my eyes and opened the Bible, then opened my eyes and read the following words:

"...and many of the apostles were imprisoned for their faith."

Later, I never could find that verse again despite Google searches and patient thumbing through the Acts of the Apostles and elsewhere.

But at the time, that little gem of inspiration was enough to lift my spirits. I recalled a song I loved in Catholic school when I was about eight years old, *Faith of our Fathers.*

"Our fathers chained in prisons dark
Were still in heart and conscience free..."

If the early Christians could endure imprisonment and other trials and tribulations, I could too.

Mary took out the lightbulb, and I lay down in the borrowed sleeping bag that had been placed on the bed for me.

"So where did you join the church?" asked Mary from the floor.

"In Australia, on holiday. How about you?"

"San Francisco. I was down by Fisherman's Wharf and this good-looking Canadian invited me to an International Dinner."

I wondered about the good-looking Canadian. *Was he why she joined?*

It was dark in that room without any lights. There was a window next to the bed, but it had been covered with construction material, preventing outside light from entering. I didn't know where I was, or how long I would be kept there. I didn't know how many other people were in the house, or who they were.

My real friends couldn't help since they didn't know where I was either. I thought about Sarah, Margaret, Pam, Chris and others, wishing I could be back at Parnell. I'd read a little about mental telepathy and figured this might be a good time to test it out. Focusing my mind as intensely as I could, I tried to convey a message to my friends:

Help, I've been kidnapped! Drive an hour north of downtown Auckland and then take a right. I'm near a beach.

5 - GOOD COP, BAD COP

The demon is a liar. He will lie to confuse us; but he will also mix lies with the truth to attack us. His attack is psychological...And powerful.
—William Peter Blatty, *The Exorcist.*

Friday, August 5, 1983

After a dreamless sleep, I woke up in the little room, which was now brightened by sunshine that made its way stubbornly through the top part of the window, above the roughly-erected construction material. While we ate, I asked Mary what "pimp" meant and she explained. Joe reappeared after breakfast to continue his verbal bombardment. If anything, he seemed meaner and more agitated than the night before, which made me nervous.

Apparently, the theme for the day was totalism. Joe was on a roll.

"Both Moon and Hitler are fanatical fascists with a lot of power over idealistic young people," he growled, half-standing, half-leaning against a chest of drawers that stood at the end of the bed.

You don't know what you're talking about.

"Their aim is to control the world, and that can only end in bloodshed."

No, you're wrong!

"What if Moon gets out the wrong side of bed one day and sends all the Moonies off to start World War Three? Isn't that why he's manufacturing M-16s, grenades and rocket launchers?"

What are you talking about? That can't be true.

"Moon is a totalist leader, a fascist like Hitler. Didn't he say, 'I will conquer and subjugate the world'?"

He didn't mean it the way you're implying.

"*You're* a totalist administrator! You're just a pimp for Moon, exploiting other people so you can get brownie points."

There he goes again with the brownie points. But something had changed. *Last night I was a mindless, unquestioning zombie and Rev. Moon was the pimp, but today, I'm the pimp. What happened? Somehow, he must have found out I'm a leader in the church, rather than one of the members.*

Then came the zinger.

"Usually the leaders have to fast a lot. You don't look as if *you* fast very much." It was a mean shot which hit me in a sensitive place.

Bastard. How dare he make comments about my weight! I seethed with hurt and indignation.

Then a woman came into the room. She was about my age but a little taller, with fair hair, blue eyes and a friendly demeanor. I guessed she was another one of Joe's recent success stories.

"Hi, I'm Rosalind." Standing near the bed, she started to tell me things that allegedly happened when she was in CARP (the student branch of the Unification Church), things obviously intended to scare me.

"Moon wanted to attach machine-guns onto fishing boats if the US wouldn't intervene in Central America." She was referring to the Sandinista revolution in Nicaragua.

"He would use armed boats manned with church members to intercept Soviet vessels carrying arms from Cuba to Nicaragua. If the fishing boats were too small, he would build larger ones."

Then Joe took the floor, straightening up to his full height as if to make his point more effectively.

"Would you kill for Reverend Moon? Doesn't the *Divine Principle* say that World War Three may have to be fought with external weapons?"

Yes, but—

Then he folded his arms defiantly, before slinging the next verbal missiles.

"Moon says, 'If I had 500 sons and daughters like you in each state, we could control the government.' If Moon told you to kill your parents, what would you do?"

That would never happen!

Up until that point, I had been trying not to dignify any of their outlandish claims with a response; but his last question was so stupid I finally lashed out.

"You're on probation!" I said, testing him. I was pretty sure I knew who he was.

"I am not on probation," he snapped back a little too quickly, scowling darkly like a guilty child.

Then, as if to show his trump card, he said something which, had it been true, might have shaken my faith right to the core.

"American ex-members say that Moon wanted three hundred good-looking sisters to do Public Relations work in Washington D.C., three for each senator. One of these PR sisters, who later left, said they were supposed to *sleep* with the senators if necessary."

I felt sick to my stomach.

I knew that at least some of what they were telling me was lies. The best way to sell a lie is to wrap it up in truth. Or, take a kernel of truth and wrap it up in lies.

Thank goodness I read The Spike*!* At one time, I had been so bewildered by Celine's irrational hatred of America, a friend had recommended *The Spike* to me, and I had learned about ideological propaganda.

They were feeding me a mixture of truths, half-truths, distortions of truth and straight-out lies, in the hope that I wouldn't know what was what; and I didn't, especially as I couldn't do any fact-checking.

Rosalind sat on the floor and leaned against the wall opposite the bed. Then a young man came in. I recognized him as one of the two from the car.

Oh no, not the singer.

He introduced himself as John, a former Unification Church member.

"Hi. Where are you from?"

"Taumaranui. I joined in America, but got sent back here with visa problems, after the wedding in Korea."

"So, you were in the October Blessing? Isn't that when Hyo-Jin was blessed?" referring to Rev. Moon's oldest son.

"Yeah, I bet he got a cute girl," he said, a little resentfully.

What's wrong, John? Wasn't your girl cute enough? Is that why you left?

Then Joe took over again, perhaps prompted by the topic of marriage.

"Moon's such a totalist jerk, he tells you who to marry! He even tells you when you can have sex! And what *position* to have it in!"

Position? There are different positions? I was intrigued, having no idea about such things. Now I wanted to get back to the church more than ever, to find out what he might be referring to.

Joe, John and Rosalind left, and a new person came into the room. He was an older man, a shorter, stockier, grayer version of Joe. I guessed he might be in his 50s, about my parents' age. Instead of towering over me like Joe usually did, the man pulled up a chair, sat on it, and smiled.

"Your family has gone through so much heartache because of you." He spoke kindly and with an American accent. "Your father is *ten* times the man Reverend Moon is!"

Who is this man and how does he know my father? Or is he just pretending that he knows my father? And why am I suddenly feeling guilty about my family?

Then I remembered that there were two Joe Alexanders in the deprogramming business, a father and a son. *This must be the father.*

The man continued chatting in a friendly manner as if we were old acquaintances.

"My nephew Biffy joined a cult called the Alamo Foundation. He completely denied his parents. He told them, 'You are just my flesh parents. Tony and Susan Alamo are my true parents.' My son and I helped get him out of there and we've been helping people ever since, to get their kids out of cults.

"Do you know there are 5000 cults in the USA? And at least 500 in Australia? Each cult is just a carbon copy of the other. The Children of God, they don't believe in thinking; at least not about anything outside their group. They say, when you think, you sink, and then you stink."

*Think, sink, stink...*I recalled my past experiences with the Children of God. When I was a student in Dunedin, I had chatted with them while shopping and ended the conversation by inviting them to dinner at my flat. On the appointed day, they showed up two hours late and with fewer people than expected, so that a lot of the food I had specially prepared for them was wasted. They certainly didn't seem to *think* much about getting to dinner on time.

"They use their women to seduce men into joining their group," the older man continued. "They call it flirty fishing. In the Children of God, any man can have any woman in the movement." Then he told me about the Love Israel cult, whose members took LSD for Holy Communion.

That was fascinating, however I didn't buy his carbon copy theory. My church didn't believe in taking any type of drugs; we didn't even use tobacco or alcohol. We lived communally but were strictly celibate until we started our married life, more like a co-ed convent than any of the odd groups he was describing. And, I thought, we would never be two hours late for a dinner appointment.

Hah! Unless we got kidnapped on the way there.

At least Joe Senior, as I began to think of him, was gentle and pleasant, unlike his son. It wasn't until much later that I realized what was going on: they were doing a good cop/bad cop routine. In this case, it was good Joe/bad Joe.

After dinner that night I was led into the living area where the television was. It was a relief to be out of the small, claustrophobic makeshift cell for a change.

My assignment was to watch a docudrama called *The Wave*, the true story of a California high school history teacher in the 1960s, who started a movement in his own classroom based on the principles behind Hitler's Youth Movement: discipline, community and action. The point was to teach his students the dangers of getting involved in a totalitarian, or totalist movement. It was a study of mob psychology in America which left me feeling unsettled. To reinforce the point, we watched a second, also disquieting film, a documentary about the SS, Hitler's Youth Army.

Then I was ushered back into my room again, with a final message for the day from the younger Joe, whom I now began to think of as Joe Junior:

"You should never allow the whole purpose concept to dominate. Never let one dictator usurp your authority over yourself. Moon and his disciples are no different from Hitler and his followers. They're both bizarre totalist organizations. Think about that."

Nice bedtime stories, Joe. Why can't you say totalitarian? Too many syllables?

That night I tried to pray and look at the Bible, but nothing really spoke to me, like on the first night. I would just have to be strong. But how long would I have to resist these people? Then I remembered about Mike Treacy's prepared breakdown. Mike had fought and argued with his captors for almost three days. On the third day, he pretended to suddenly "snap" into a great epiphany in which he denounced his faith. Over the following days and weeks, he was able to win the trust of his deprogrammers and plan his escape. The thought of it made me smile as I lay down in the darkness.

I would borrow Mike's clever strategy. Day One was over; two more to go.

6 – "LOVE ME, I'M SATAN!"

I cannot, and I will not retract, for it is unsafe for a Christian to speak against his conscience.

— Martin Luther

August 6, 1983

It was Saturday morning, Day Two, inside the house of felons, ex-members and other perpetrators. If my mother was still around, there were eight of us: seven against one, and I was their prisoner.

I was not beaten, raped or physically abused. I had food, drink, shelter and *accompanied* bathroom access; yet I was like a captive creature in a circus or zoo. It was intolerable. They'd forced me there against my will and were keeping me, not telling me if or when I would ever be able to leave.

I feared if I were to vent my anger and frustration, that they would use it against me. I determined to remain calm and rational to withstand whatever imaginative garbage they had prepared for me. I was sitting on the edge of the bed eating breakfast when Joe Junior strode in, briefcase in hand, and started up. I kept eating, but inwardly prayed, bracing for the impact.

Lord, place a hedge of protection around my mind and heart.

To all his rantings, I would find defiant rebuttals and *think* them quietly. There was no point arguing with someone whose business was to promote evil lies and outrageous propaganda.

"Many American members who joined ten years ago became disillusioned when Moon came to America." Joe sat awkwardly on a wooden chair, long limbs bending at the joints and shoulders stooping.

A giant grasshopper with a moustache and an American accent...

"They didn't like his methods. After editing the *Divine Principle*, one brother left the movement, dissatisfied. The Principle had lost its mystique for him."

Oh really, someone left without any help? He didn't have to be kidnapped? Perhaps he was capable of independent thinking.

"Another didn't like Moon's emphasis on fundraising, purchasing of real estate and influencing of academics and politicians, like Nixon."

Sounds like an ex-hippy who still wasn't grounded.

Joe spat out the word "Nixon" as though it left a bad taste in his mouth. If ever there was a more hated politician, I don't know who it was. I could still remember watching his 1974 resignation speech on the TV in my parents' living room, in my school uniform. I was 16. He looked so distraught, I felt sorry for him. Rev Moon had seen that the embattled Nixon could protect America against Communism, and he organized campaigns urging Americans to forgive, love and unite.

"Moon hates homosexuals," Joe continued, unrelenting. "When a member had a homosexual problem, Moon said, 'If it causes a problem, cut it off and barbecue it. Put it in a shoe-box and send it to me'." I cringed involuntarily.

How horrible!

My pulse rate was increasing. I felt my stomach squirm. From the context it was clear that 'it' referred to the penis of the brother struggling with homosexual feelings. *Did Joe make this up?* It was like a scene from a dark Korean mobster movie and I couldn't believe Joe had that much imagination. More likely, Rev Moon *had* said it, possibly tongue-in-cheek, to address a thorny issue mostly unheard-of in his native Korea at that time.

"Also, sick members were sent home to their parents, abandoned."

Isn't that your goal, to get all the Moonies back to their parents? Shouldn't you be happy about that?

Joe reached into his loaded briefcase, took out some typed and stapled sheets of paper and started reading excerpts from the testimony of Judy Stanley, a horse trainer.

"Stanley alleges that Moon's children were so spoiled that one sister was given $12,000 to buy horses for them *and* she was given hundreds of dollars every week to buy McDonalds and Kentucky Fried Chicken."

So what? He has a lot of children. And horses are expensive.

"One day she chastised Hyo-Jin (eldest son of Rev and Mrs. Moon) for being cruel to the horses. She slapped him and then was severely chastised herself."

Perhaps she lost her temper and was out of line.

"Hyo-Jin upset some of the members by shooting squirrels. He often came out of the woods, dragging dead animals."

So what? It's called hunting...

Joe put the testimony back in his briefcase and closed it, then began to extemporize, gradually raising his volume.

"Hyo-Jin was recently busted for possession of marijuana. He was expelled from his private school for fighting. If Moon's the messiah, how come he can't even control his own kids?"

Perhaps because they have free will?

"Moon has five cars for his personal use, including a custom-made Lincoln Continental. He eats from gold-etched dishes that get thrown away after he's finished, since he's not supposed to eat out of used dishes."

That's ridiculous. I don't believe it.

"He was seen with his wife and the Dursts at a casino in Vegas, *gambling.* He can't be the messiah. A messiah doesn't do things like that."

How would you know? Do you make the rules?

"He's just a jerk."

No, he's a man of God and you're *the jerk!*

"He's just another fanatic totalist leader like Charlie Manson, Jim Jones or Hitler. Those science conferences and relief organizations are just for PR, so he can clean up his act and be accepted by the National Council of Churches."

And your cynicism knows no bounds.

"Why is Moon's son allowed to have a rock band when the members are not allowed to listen to rock music?"

I don't know, and I don't care.

"Why is Moon's daughter Ye-Jin allowed to have long hair worn loose, when the church sisters are not supposed to?"

Don't know, don't care.

"What kind of messiah makes false prophesies? Moon said there had to be a certain number of people at that Yankee Stadium rally, and if there were fewer, even *one* less, Satan would claim the victory. There were *many* less, but he still said it was a victory."

I don't know! Perhaps there was a different kind of victory, like keeping faith through that thunderstorm?

"Moon's first wife openly denounces him. He tells everyone she's scrubbing floors in Korea in repentance, but that's not even true. She's living in California."

I don't know anything about her. Maybe she's scrubbing floors in California? Why should I believe any of this?

Joe reopened the briefcase, his eyelids heavy as though he were tired or bored; but below the drooping lids there was a gleam of anticipation as if he had a trump card to pull out.

And he did. Joe played his hand well, producing transcripts from the recent Tony Colombrito court case in New York City, in which Rev Moon himself had been called to testify.

"Moon stated under oath that he had an illegitimate child by a Miss Kim in North Korea while still married to his first wife." I froze, my heart pounding.

What? No! That can't be true.

"He was a bigamist! A cheater!"

No!

Joe held the court transcripts in front of my face, so I could see for myself. There it was in black and white, with yellow highlighter to emphasize the most incriminating, most devastating sentences. It seemed genuine, like a photocopy of an official document.

How can this be? Could Father have committed adultery, the worst sin? That's unthinkable, unimaginable! Is this a terrible scandal that's been deliberately covered up? Or is there some deeper, more thoughtful explanation?

The information hit me like a punch to the gut, and I could feel my lower lip quivering, my eyes starting to tear up. Joe was in his element, and now standing triumphantly, he began preaching like the devil.

"Dr Shin testified that the original blood-cleansing involved sexual rites between Moon and his female followers. Having sex with Moon was supposed to purify their lineage."

Stop! That's disgusting, and I don't believe it!

"That's why people were found dancing in the nude. This was mentioned in *Time* magazine. If it wasn't true, why didn't Moon speak out or take legal action?"

I don't know!

"He said each woman received a personal revelation to dance in the nude. That just lacks credibility. How would each person get the exact same revelation?"

I don't know! Please stop! I've heard enough already.

"Think about that! You owe it to yourself."

Okay, dummy. If ritual sex and naked dancing were such an important part of my religion, why have I never, ever been invited to such events in almost seven years of membership? I never heard of such crazy carrying-on in any Unification Church in the whole world.

Joe left the room after handing off the briefcase to the ever-cheerful Joe Senior, who came in, followed by Mary. He sat in the chair, she on the floor.

"How are you doing today?" he asked, getting comfortable in the chair, but not waiting for an answer. "Your brother sure is tall. He should be playing basketball! I told him that, but he's never been all that interested."

What? My brother's here too? Another invisible punch hit my midsection.

"He and my younger son, Jerry, have been doing night duty outside the room here." He beamed with pride as though they were Eagle Scouts earning their Kidnap Assistant Merit Badges. I guessed Jerry was the other guy from the car, who had remained nameless until now, at least in my mind.

My brother was 19 and going to school in Dunedin. He was a good kid; I could hardly believe he'd been roped into this awful situation.

When I tuned back in to Joe, he was boasting about his deprogramming career.

"...we've had approximately a 96 per cent success rate. Recently I got an Australian kid, Gil Alexander, out."

How sad.

"He'd been in that wedding at Madison Square Garden."

You mean, my *wedding?*

"He and his wife, Nina, were considered the 'ideal Moonie couple'. I deprogrammed Gil and then Gil got Nina out."

How dare you! Those are my Blessing alumni!

"Then there was Rick Lamartina. He felt rebuffed by his Japanese wife after she listened to a lecture on lustful Americans. And Lyall Jones, another Australian...he recently appeared on *60 Minutes*, or was it *Four Corners*?"

Gil, Nina, Rick, Lyall...how depressing. How sad.

"Gary Scharff was another one. He used to be a lecturer at Barrytown and Boonville. Now he's an authority on mind control techniques and does deprogrammings with his wife."

Wow, what a career choice.

"She wrote the book *Hostage to Heaven,* about the Faithful Five, who all left the Oakland family around the same time and now help in deprogrammings."

What, they left the Oakland family by themselves? They didn't need your help, or their mommies and daddies?

"I was in the Oakland church," added Mary, her face still not betraying any emotion. "Kristina always slept on a bed, while the other sisters slept on the floor. She got a back-rub every morning."

Kristina...that name came up before. She was the one who "invented" the mind-control techniques! She must be a special person to be so maligned. I hope I get to meet her someday.

"Dr Durst is only a Junior High School teacher," Joe reminded me. "He's not a PhD. And his wife, she's supposedly sick with T.B. but she's always out on shopping sprees. Says she's doing PR but has nothing to show for it. Tells the members to practice 'heavenly deception', where you lie about stuff but it's okay, because you're lying for God."

Sure, Joe! The biggest liar is you! Liar, liar, pants on fire!

"West Garden, where the Dursts live, is luxurious," said Mary, in a monotone.

Good. I hope I get to see it someday.

"There's a golden crown there from Korea that's worth one million dollars. Onni (Mrs. Durst) was always 'clunking' people on the third eye if they were sleepy, or if she thought they were off-center, possessed or something."

"Yeah," added Joe, "she's a strange woman. One person saw her with six shopping bags full of the members' fundraising money. And she told a sister to lock up Durst's children in a closet."

Right, Joe. It's always the best people that are the most misunderstood and misrepresented. She's probably a living saint.

"I have a testimony here by Renee Dunkley. She says Onni accused her of being to blame for her brother's death. 'Because of your unrighteousness, your brother had to die.' Then some other bad thing happened to Renee's family and Onni said, 'How many more lives do you want to destroy through your unrighteousness?' One member was told, 'God will cast you out forever.'"

Apostates and atrocity stories, Joe. It's so cliché. But why does it make me feel nervous and uncomfortable?

"Before I joined the church," Mary shared, "I was down near Fisherman's Wharf in San Francisco and I met this good-looking Canadian guy."

The Canadian. She's mentioned him before.

"He asked me to come and find out about the *Creative Community Project*. It sounded interesting and he seemed nice. I went to their weekend workshop in Boonville, but I didn't know it was a religion. I never even heard of Moon until I was already on a fundraising team."

Maybe you didn't ask the good-looking Canadian enough questions.

Later that day I was escorted into the living room to watch a movie called *Ticket to Heaven.* A young man called David joins a new religious group based in San Francisco. He first attends their workshop in the mountains, where a hyper-enthusiastic young woman leads mandatory songs, games and group exercises, and an awkward-looking man in business attire gives lectures with an odd British accent. Food is mostly some sort of gruel and peer pressure is enormous. David graduates from the camp and goes to the city. A tall, charismatic woman with glassy eyes runs the communal house where he stays.

Is this Kristina?

David's close friend, alarmed at his long absence and the sudden change in his personality, convinces David's family that he is in a destructive cult. Family and friends travel from Toronto to help kidnap him. They hire a deprogrammer who is tall, lean and arrogant.

Pretty obvious who that *is!*

About ten people wait outside a bedroom while the man works on David. It all looks uncomfortably familiar. The deprogrammer yells, menaces and ridicules. At one point he jumps on top of David (who is lying down) shouting, "Love me! I'm Satan. You're supposed to love your enemy. How come you don't love me?"

What a freak! This is supposed to be therapy? He'd better not try that on me.

After many days of this treatment, David gives in and breaks down, weeping, and realizes he has been deceived and manipulated. His family and friends embrace him, and the story ends with a group hug.

The movie was disturbing and weird. If I was supposed to see myself in it, I didn't. Something which nobody in that house seemed to understand or appreciate was that *my* experience of joining the

Unification Church was not at all like the movie, and not at all like the so-called Oakland experience that was being depicted by Mary. It was *so* different, it felt like we hadn't even joined the same movement.

7 - TANYA

How beautiful upon the mountains are the feet of him who brings good tidings, who publishes peace, who brings good tidings of good, who publishes salvation.
—Isaiah 52:7

January 1977

The day I met Tanya was one of those pivotal days which happen rarely in a life-time yet open a whole new realm of possibilities.

I was walking down the Rundle Mall in Adelaide, South Australia, eating a pear. It was late morning, and already hot. Diane, my flat-mate from Dunedin, and I were job-hunting and thought we might have more success if we split up.

We had landed in Sydney in December, then spent a few weeks in Queensland.

Someone had told us that Adelaide was the place to visit, and for some reason we both felt a strong inclination to go there, even though it was over 1200 miles away. So, we did what came naturally to moderately adventurous 19-year-old college students on a limited budget: we put on our backpacks, stuck out our thumbs and hitchhiked out of Queensland, across New South Wales and all the way to South Australia.

Adelaide was called the City of Churches, which sounded good to me, and I felt more comfortable there than I had in the bustling, over-commercialized Gold Coast. With a population of about a million, it was the fifth most populous city in Australia. We found a youth hostel near the city center and settled in.

The Central Business District of Adelaide is laid out like a grid, with Rundle Mall as its centerpiece. The Mall was Australia's first pedestrian street mall and had only been open a few months by the time we arrived.

A tall, heavy-set woman approached me. She was wearing a skirt, short-sleeved blouse and a panama hat. I guessed she was in her twenties. Pinned to her blouse was a round badge which bore a red symbol on a white background: a circle enclosing a square, with rays emanating from a smaller circle inside the square. Around the edge of the symbol I could see the words "Holy Spirit Association for the Unification of World Christianity" (the official name of the Unification Church).

I had never heard of it.

"Hi!" she said enthusiastically. "Would you like to see some changes in the world?"

Would I ever.

Aloud, I said, "Yes, I'd like to see more Christianity and more ecumenism." (My experiences in Dunedin had led me to hope that people might take religion more seriously if religious people themselves could get along; therefore, I was interested in the modern ecumenical movement.)

"My name's Tanya," she said with a big smile. "Let's go and talk some more." She handed me a pamphlet and started walking. I followed, thinking we would sit down somewhere in the Mall. As we chatted, we quickly discovered that both of us were New Zealanders. After a month in Australia I was already homesick, and it was a huge comfort to meet a nice, friendly kiwi.

We didn't sit down in the Rundle Mall. Tanya kept walking and I kept following. "I'm supposed to be job-hunting," I protested, mildly.

"Well, mornings are better for job-hunting," she responded, and since it was close to noon, I thought her point was reasonable.

"Where are we going?"

"Almost there," she said cheerfully.

After about ten minutes we reached a modest, one-storied house on Wakefield Street, near the eastern edge of the business district, and coincidentally, a short walk from the youth hostel where Diane and I were staying. There was another one of those red-on-white symbols on the outside of the building. *The Holy Spirit Association*...I reckoned if it had something to do with the Holy Spirit, it must be okay. She opened the front door and led me into a sparsely-furnished room. There was a medium sized table set with drink coasters and surrounded with foldable wooden chairs. The floor was covered with sea-grass matting. The place was simple, but spotlessly clean. There were posters on the wall, but I paid little attention to them.

"What would you like to drink?" asked Tanya. "Tea, coffee, water, orange juice, lemonade, iced coffee, iced tea, iced Milo?"

It was hard to choose from such a generous menu, but I managed to decide.

"An iced coffee would be lovely." Tanya nodded eagerly and disappeared for a while. I sat down on one of the wooden chairs.

As I sat gratefully sipping the cool, sweet drink, Tanya asked me my thoughts about God.

"Well, God is love, God is all-powerful and all-knowing," I began and beyond that, I didn't know much about the creator of the universe, despite my intensive religious education. I imagined Him to be some formless, infinite blob of energy somewhere in the cosmos. But I wanted to know more, and it seemed I had come to the right place.

"God has an external form and an internal character. Everything is made in God's image and everything in the creation also has internal character and external form. For example, mind and body. God also has masculinity and femininity."

That sounded reasonable and besides, she was so nice, I just wanted to hear what she had to say.

She put some sheets of blank paper in front of her and began drawing diagrams. The first was a yin-yang symbol. She drew a plus sign and a minus sign on it, to indicate masculine and feminine.

God represented by a yin-yang sign...that was radical. Revolutionary.

In Catholic doctrine, the symbol typically used for God was a triangle, representing the Holy Trinity: Father, Son and Holy Spirit, an all-male threesome. Yet Tanya was implying that God was at least half *female*, at least he/she had to be, to be accurately reflected in the things of creation which, she pointed out, were ALL created in pairs.

"Even atoms have protons and electrons. Molecules are made of cations and anions. Everything exists through reciprocal relationships."

"Yes, that's true."

I had never thought of myself as a feminist, yet something inside me resonated with what Tanya was saying. It made such perfect sense that God would possess femininity, that I wondered why I'd never thought of it before.

Soon Tanya had made enough lines and circles on the page to create four diamond shaped diagrams, representing the Three Great Blessings: "Be fruitful, multiply and have dominion" (Genesis 1:28). Being fruitful meant an individual's body and mind uniting, centered on God. Multiplying meant perfected man and perfected woman uniting centered on God and producing godly offspring. Dominion meant perfected humans exercising a dominion of love over the creation.

Finally, Tanya told me it was God's original ideal to live in harmony with humankind and the creation. She drew another diagram, this time with three of those awesome yin-yang symbols in one vertical line. The top one represented God, the middle one people and the bottom one, the creation. Then with her pencil she began drawing a figure eight that turned into a kind of double helix. It started from God, went around the people, reached down to the creation, and as she kept retracing it over and over, she was telling me that this was the original ideal: God, humankind and the creation united together in love and harmony.

I was enthralled. I'd never heard anything like that in my life.

"Would you like to come back another time and hear more?" Tanya asked.

There's more?

"Sure, I'll come back tomorrow about two o'clock."

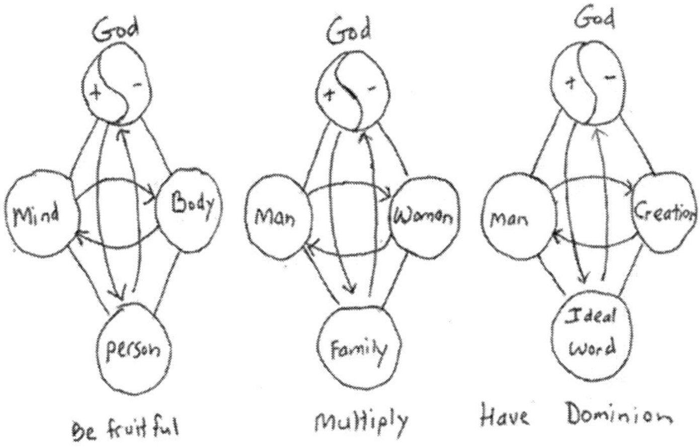

The Three Great Blessings

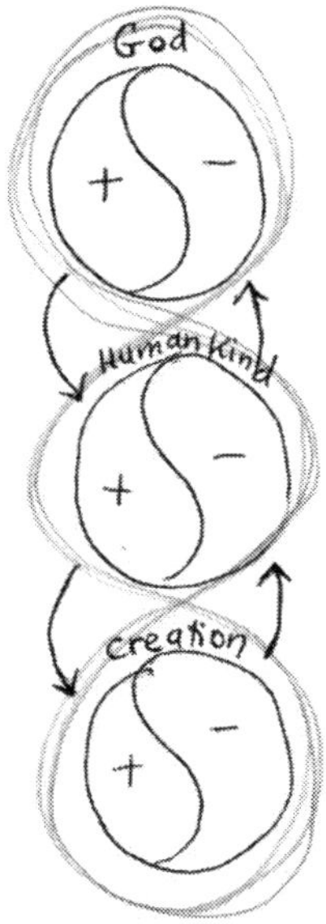

The Double Helix

8 - PARADISE REGAINED

Long is the way and hard that out of hell leads up to light.
—John Milton, *Paradise Lost*

I went back to the house the next day to hear more, as planned. Tanya looked happy to see me again and introduced me to an Australian woman who looked about the same age as Tanya (which I guessed to be early to mid-twenties), but fairer and smaller in stature. Her name was Sue.

"I'll be teaching you tonight," said Sue. There was something in Sue's tone and demeanor that impressed me immediately. She was kind yet serious, humble yet confident. She had an air of quiet reverence, not unlike some of the Dominican Sisters I knew and loved.

"What would you like to drink?" asked Tanya. "Tea, coffee, water, lemonade, orange juice, iced tea, iced coffee, iced Milo?"

Hmmm...what should I try today?

"I think I'll have the lemonade."

Sue and I sat down at opposite sides of the table and she picked up some sheets of paper and a pencil, placing them in front of her.

After reviewing the material that I had already heard from Tanya, Sue started talking about the Original Sin. She said the story about the Fall of Man in the Book of Genesis was symbolic; for example, the serpent symbolized Satan, a creature formerly known as Lucifer. That was a familiar concept to me from my recent study of Milton's *Paradise Lost.* One of my English essays had been on the Fall of Man. I remembered Lucifer as the powerful, charismatic archangel who had said, "Better to reign in Hell than serve in Heaven."

Sue said that the two trees in the Garden of Eden represented man and woman, and the fruit represented the love of a woman. The Knowledge of Good and Evil symbolized something like carnal knowledge; eating the fruit represented an act of fornication, or sexual sin. That sounded reasonable to me, more sensible than sin coming into the world by somebody eating an apple.

Tanya returned with a tall glass of ice-cold lemonade, then pulled up a chair next to us at the table.

Sue was drawing more circles, lines and diamonds, but this time, instead of the Three Blessings, it was the Three Adams. "The first man and woman fell from grace, bringing sin into the world and becoming the false parents of humankind."

Paradise Lost.

"The Second Adam was Jesus, who came to restore what Adam had lost."

Paradise Regained.

"Jesus should have married," Sue was saying.

Jesus should have married! Wow. That was radical, but not entirely new to me. Malcolm Muggeridge in *Jesus Rediscovered* had imagined Jesus praying in Gethsemane, wishing he could live a normal life, go back to his hometown and marry one of the village girls. How desirable that was, but how impossible.

"Jesus didn't come to die," she said.

What?

"Jesus should have married, but he willingly died on the cross as a sacrifice for sinners, due to the faithlessness of the Jewish people. Since Satan exercised his maximum power to kill Jesus, God could use His maximum power to resurrect him."

I recalled the mysterious writing on the Stone Table in C.S. Lewis' *Chronicles of Narnia*. Aslan, by means of the Deeper Magic from before the dawn of time, overcomes death.

"Because Jesus had no bride, God sent the Holy Spirit as a spiritual bride," Sue was saying.

"Through uniting with the resurrected Jesus and the Holy Spirit, we are 'born again' and receive spiritual salvation. We are still waiting for complete salvation, which will be possible through the Second Advent."

Every few sentences she would look up from the paper and make eye contact with me, to make sure I was following, and I would nod, once again spellbound.

It made sense. We need two parents to be born, therefore we need two spiritual parents to be reborn, a male and a female. *Of course! Why hadn't I thought of that before?* I loved the logic and the symmetry of it.

"At the Second Advent, the Third Adam will appear, along with a Third Eve," she continued. "Together, they will fully restore the original ancestors. They will be the True Parents of humankind."

Paradise Completely Regained.

That made sense. Obviously, the world wasn't completely restored. That would happen at the Second Advent.

Tanya refreshed my drink and brought a glass of water for Sue.

"This is just skeletal information," said Sue. "We can go into it in greater depth after I've given you an overview. Shall we continue?"

It was a lot to take in, but I was eager to hear more.

She then taught me about the Providence of Restoration, explaining how the events of human history are shaped by God's efforts to reclaim the world which He created, and return it to its original state. The central characters of the Old Testament were key players who helped advance the providence by setting conditions of faith.

By the time Moses appeared, God had established a chosen people, the Israelites, based on conditions of faith successfully laid by their forefathers Abraham, Isaac and Jacob.

Sue then divided the history of ancient Israel into six distinct periods, thereby presenting the clearest and most succinct overview of the Old Testament I had ever heard in my life. I was impressed, but what I heard next completely blew my mind.

She had already drawn a tall rectangular column divided into six sections, representing Old Testament history. Now she was placing a second column beside the first, to represent the New Testament era. I was in awe when she showed that there was a parallel period in New Testament history for each period of the Old. They were approximately the same lengths. For example, there was a 400-year period of persecution suffered by early Christians, which paralleled the 400 years of slavery in Egypt, and so on.

According to the timeline, we were living in the time of the Second Advent, a time parallel to the birth of Jesus.

That was the best news I had heard in a long time. I had been wondering about the Second Coming, and now these people were telling me it could happen in our lifetimes. This was staggering. All this information, and the way it fitted together and made sense...it was as if someone had cracked a secret code.

I was excited to see the patterns in human history, which proved that history was not random, but was the manifestation of Divine Providence. Suddenly God became more real than ever.

But something else had happened that was life-changing. While discussing New Testament history, Sue had explained that during the Middle Ages, the Catholic Church had become corrupt, much like the Kings of Israel in the Old Testament. God had sent special people to call the church to repentance, such as Francis of Assisi; however, the corruption continued. By the 1500s Martin Luther was called to reform the church, and in the conflict that followed, Catholicism stood in the Cain position (further from God) while Protestantism was in the Abel position (closer to God).

From that day on, I no longer wished to consider myself a Catholic.

9 - SUN MYUNG MOON

The world has known many saviors. The very word savior means healer. Mr. Moon is one who is to heal not simply the bodies, but the minds and the spirits of men. And when a person is healed, he is free.
–Arthur Ford, *Unknown but Known*

I kept going back to the center for a few hours each time, hungry to hear more of this Divine Principle that was re-explaining my faith to me and taking it to a whole new level of understanding. I didn't know what I might do with all this information. I certainly wanted to share it with my Catholic friends and family. Surely, they would be as amazed as I was. Perhaps I could go back to Dunedin and turn my flat into a Divine Principle teaching center. I imagined putting one of those red and white signs in the window of my Clarendon Street living room. I wondered what reaction it might get.

One thing was for sure: after hearing all this shocking new information, I was on a whole new track in my spiritual journey. There would be no turning back.

One day we were studying the Second Coming, a topic which intrigued me. In Dunedin I had discussions with Jehovah's Witnesses and Children of God to find out what they knew. I lost interest in the Witnesses when they informed me that the Catholic Church was the Whore of Babylon in the Book of Revelation. I was disappointed in the Children of God and their Comet Kahoutek comic books when they showed up two hours late for a dinner appointment at my flat. But Sue was always respectful and reverent. What she told me was fascinating, and it made sense.

She taught me that Christ was a mission rather than a person, and that Jesus of Galilee was a person anointed with that mission. But Jesus himself would not return. Rather, another person would be born on earth who would inherit the mission of Christ, in the same manner that John the Baptist inherited the spirit of Elijah. That same person would also be a great teacher and a revealer of New Truth.

"New Truth? You mean, like the *Divine Principle*?"

"Yes," said Sue.

"So, the person who revealed the *Divine Principle* is the new Christ?"

"That's what we believe."

"So, who is that person?"

"His name is Sun Myung Moon."

Then Sue presented an account of Sun Myung Moon's life, as taught by his early disciples. I listened eagerly as she read to me about a young boy of 16, who met Jesus on a Korean mountainside one Easter Morning, and consequently devoted his entire life to the work of God's kingdom. I heard about dreadful persecution by numerous governments. As a young student in Japan he was tortured by Japanese colonial police, who suspected him of being a Communist. He was arrested twice by North Korean authorities on charges of disturbing the peace and being a swindler. On the second occasion, he was found guilty and sentenced to five years in a Communist labor camp, escaping only because the Korean War had begun, and UN forces were advancing on the camp. After the Korean War ended, he began a ministry in South Korea, where he was arrested by South Korean authorities for allegedly evading the draft. At one point he was tortured and beaten so badly that the police threw his lifeless body out into the snow. Grieving disciples recovered the body and miraculously nursed him back to health with Chinese herbs. After three days, he recovered. That was profoundly meaningful to me. *Three days, just like the three days Jesus lay in his tomb before the resurrection.*

It was an extraordinary account of an extraordinary man. He was greater than Malcolm Muggeridge or even Mother Theresa. I felt he was the kind of person that appears only once in a lifetime, or perhaps only once in a millennium.

At that moment, I first believed that Sun Myung Moon was the new Christ. I was so excited, I wanted to shout it from the rooftops. But Sue advised caution. She explained that just as Jesus was heavily persecuted by the religious leaders of his time, Rev Moon was still being opposed by powerful leaders in the Christian world, who failed to understand and believe him.

From that time on, I had the distinct feeling that God was not only calling Sun Myung Moon. He was also calling me. It was a feeling of great responsibility. I felt like Noah, when he was called to build the ark. Noah probably asked, "Who, me? Are you sure?" which was my reaction. Sue asked me if I prayed. I said yes. I needed to pray about this. I asked God, "What is it you want me to do?"

Around that time, several things happened. I had my first taste of persecution when I mentioned to some travelers at my youth hostel that I was studying at the Unification Church. They were a Canadian couple, a bearded man and his curvaceous bottle-blonde girlfriend. They were Christians. Sometimes they joked about the other Canadian hostellers behind their backs, two nice women whom they referred to as "Goofy Noofies" because they were from Newfoundland.

"Oh, that's the Moonies!" they said. "We have them all over the US. They're in Canada too. They're brainwashed zombies and their leader is the anti-Christ."

That being a new perspective I hadn't considered, I encouraged them to come to the center with me and tell Sue what they'd told me. I wanted to hear her response.

That night, all three of us went over to the center. Sue's response was to patiently and respectfully try to teach them an outline of the *Divine Principle*. They were unimpressed and eventually left. I asked Sue, "How can you know if someone is the Christ or the anti-Christ?"

Unflinching, Sue looked directly into my eyes and said, "You will know them by their fruits. Good fruit cannot come from a bad tree."

It was a wise answer. I hadn't met many of the "fruits" of Rev Moon, just Tanya, Sue and a couple of others who lived at the center. But I sensed that their lifestyle was pure and holy, more than mine was and probably more than those nay-saying Canadians.

One Sunday, I attended church service at the center. Usually I attended Mass. Although it was the first time in my life, I went to a non-Catholic service instead of Mass, I felt absolutely no pangs of conscience, as though this was where God wanted me to be. That was when I first heard the most wonderful songs, "Holy Songs", about the suffering heart of God as He struggled for eons to restore humanity to His bosom.

How many fathoms deep is His aching heart?
All the tears He shed for earth became an endless sea.

I knew for a certainty that no anti-Christ could write songs like that, nor could the followers of an anti-Christ. Those songs had to have come straight from heaven.

But what did God want me to do about that?

I had a part-time job as a waitress at the Norwood Hotel in North Adelaide. One night I had a dream that Reverend Moon came into the kitchen of the hotel, where I was depositing dirty dishes after bussing tables. He was wearing a western-style business suit like in some of the posters I'd seen at the center, and he just looked at me and smiled. He didn't say the words, "Drop your dishes and follow me," but that was what I sensed. It was like when Jesus told the fishermen to leave their nets.

One night I had dinner at the center. "We live simply," Sue said. The food was simple, but nutritious and beautifully presented: white rice and a fillet of baked fish with steamed vegetables. Afterward we had a segment of rock-melon for dessert. I helped clear the table and noticed in the kitchen a small chalkboard with names on it. I was surprised to see my name on there. "Is that a list of who's coming to dinner?" I asked. "No," said Tanya, "that's our prayer list." I was astonished. I was on their prayer list? They were praying for me? It was amazing to think of that. Was that why I'd had that dream?

As we relaxed after the meal, I expressed my appreciation to Sue and the others for their hospitality and for all they'd done for me. Then Sue dropped the bombshell. "Would you like to help us?"

"Help *you?* How would I help you? You're the ones who've been helping me."

She explained that I could move in with them and help them to teach and spread the *Divine Principle* to others. They were asking me to join them and live with them.

At first, I couldn't think of it. I was due to go home to New Zealand in just over a week and get ready to go back to school. What would my parents say? What would my friends think?

"I can't *not* go home," I protested.

"Just try it for a while and see how you like it," Sue suggested. That sounded reasonable. I moved in that same night. It was just a trial period.

While staying in the center I was able to pray more about what I should do. Not going home at first seemed impossible. Then one night, while showering, I suddenly saw a different perspective. Yes, it would be hard to not go home and no doubt there would be resistance and opposition. But I suddenly felt, years from now, future generations would look back and appreciate my decision. I needed to look at the bigger picture.

I'd figured it out. The "ark" I was being asked to build was to become a missionary of the Unification Church. I said Yes.

When God wants to make a revelation...He has to choose a human instrument, who, through some circumstances or conditions, has been brought to the point of sensitiveness and spiritual perception so that he can, in his own person, accept this ancient light of wisdom - and through him it will filter down to others. ...

—Arthur C. Ford

Reverend and Mrs. Moon
Children's Day - 1985

10 - "A COGENT THESIS"

Course nobody can understand the damn thing [Divine Principle]. That's the whole idea. [They] never read it. It's all just a pile of junk.
—Joe "Franklin", one of the deprogrammers in Ted Patrick's *Let Our Children Go.*

Sunday, August 7, 1983

It was Day Three, and I was anxious. This was the day I planned to fake my breakdown, as my friend Mike had done so well. In the bathroom, as I showered and dressed, with Mary there watching quietly as always, I tried to recall more of Mike's story.

That's right! He got so friendly with his deprogramming team that he helped them work on their car. When he was done, he offered to take it for a test drive. They let him, and he drove more than sixty miles, to the nearest police station!

What a great story it was! If only I could do something like that...but I didn't have mechanical skills, or a driver's license. I wondered if the police were looking for me, or if anyone was trying to find me. But then, why should they? I got myself into this mess, I should get myself out. I would do the prepared breakdown thing, then figure out the rest.

Joe was in a worse mood than ever. He looked tired and frustrated and acted like he was disgusted with me. He was ridiculing the *Divine Principle* in his rough, mean, rasping voice.

"A lot of things in the *Principle* are inconsistent with the Bible. Adam and Eve were already husband and wife before the Fall, so why was it a sin to have sex?"

What? They were? I don't know...

"Noah built the ark for 100 years, not 120."

Really?

"There were 990 years between Adam and Noah, not 1600."

There must be some explanation...

"Jacob was in Haran for 20 years, not 21."

Maybe it was 20.5 and they rounded it off to the nearest whole number?

"So obviously, *Divine Principle* contradicts the Bible! It's full of half-truths and inconsistencies."

No, it's not! How dare you be so disrespectful!

The *Principle* had changed my life for the better. It was a beautiful teaching. The more he attacked it, the more offended I felt.

You are a big bully and your voice is getting on my nerves! If a tumor could talk, it would sound like you! Why should I even listen to your sacrilege?

I lay down on the bed with my hands over my ears, trying to block the sound of his mocking.

It didn't help. He just shouted louder.

"Open your mind! Stop being a willing slave and start thinking for yourself! Think, Maree, think! The truth will set you free."

All right, I'll show you! I'll prove *there's nothing wrong with my mind. You're going to get a piece of it!*

I sat up on the bed and glared at him, ready for a fight.

What have you got, Bozo? Bring it on.

"The notion of building an ideal world is unrealistic. It's ridiculous. This world isn't so bad. There's a lot of good people out there, it's not all Satanic. You people are just paranoid."

"Just because you're paranoid, doesn't mean they're not out to get you," I shot back. It was a joke I'd heard years before, and I couldn't resist. It was so fitting.

Joe didn't appreciate my sense of humor.

"Smart-ass."

He should have been glad that he'd finally coerced me into a conversation, if you could call it that.

"The *Divine Principle*," Joe said, his voice sour with contempt, "is not even original."

So??

"Hell, we've got a legal document from the Monastery of Israel in Korea. They say they knew that same shit decades before Moon started teaching it."

That suggests its validity, you moron.

"All of Chapter One, all of Chapter Two, that wasn't Moon's. It was written by a dude named Baek-Moon Kim, leader of the Israel Monastery."

So?? They agreed on some things. Fascinating.

"Moon stole it from them."

No, he didn't.

"Same thing with that 'Inside Belly Church'. Their leader had the same so-called revelations that Moon had. He just took over their leadership and 'borrowed' their teachings." Joe added an extra heaping of sarcasm to the last few sentences.

(In 1946 many Christian groups in Korea were expecting the Second Coming to happen in their country. One such group was led by a Mrs. Ho, whose belly would contract whenever she received revelations from Jesus. This was a sign that the new Messiah would be born on earth through a woman.)

"Well, doesn't that confirm the validity of the revelations, since other people were 'getting' the same thing, like they were on the same wavelength?" I suggested, hopefully.

"It doesn't confirm *nothin'*. It's pseudo-scientific junk. Take the dual characteristics thing. Not every organism multiplies through give-and-take action between positive and negative. How about an *amoeba?*"

Um...

"And that Four Position Foundation, that can't be the absolute ideal for everyone. What if you're single? Childless? Homosexual?"

Well...

"Oh yeah, if you're gay, you have to cut it off, barbecue it and send it to him in a shoebox. That's so bizarre."

Not that again, please...

Joe was nit-picking. If he hoped to break me by attempting to disprove, dismantle and ridicule the *Divine Principle,* I didn't like his chances.

Since first hearing the teaching in 1977 I had thoroughly examined the *Divine Principle Study Guide*, read the 'Black Book' ten times, the *Level Four* version four times as well as all six volumes of the *Home Study Guide.* I had taught and frequently defended it to probably hundreds of people. I could teach an overview with pencil and paper as Sue and Tanya had done; I could teach from a binder or an oversized art pad with diagrams beautifully pre-drawn. I could lecture on blackboard, whiteboard, two-hour version, six-hour version, weekend seminar; or the five-minute version on paper napkins in a café, whatever the situation required. I felt confident.

Also, people a lot smarter than me were impressed by *Divine Principle.* In 1981 I had a Home Church area in Sydney. (Home Church is a missionary activity in which a member adopts a neighborhood of 360 homes which they visit regularly and try to serve unconditionally.) In my area, which was across the street from the church center in Randwick, there lived a small community of Catholic brothers from the order of De La Salles, a teaching congregation founded in France. Brothers Max, Marty and John became good neighbors and good friends. They would come to our center for meals or lectures and we would attend Masses at their house. I once lent my copy of *Level Four Divine Principle* to Brother Marty who, after a careful reading, declared it "a cogent thesis."

In contrast, it occurred to me that Joe came across as a hater of religion, which didn't seem right. If someone is *hired* to talk another person out of their faith, shouldn't he be an expert on matters of religion? Or if not religion, how about psychology? Yet Joe seemed like neither a person of faith nor a mental health professional.

Used car salesman, Chris had said.

"Do you even know anything about religion?" I blurted out.

"Yeah," he replied in his slow drawl. "I was into Buddhism."

I had to suppress an urge to laugh out loud, not only at the idea of Joe as a Buddhist, but also the way he said it, like "Boo-dism".

Joe, you're the rudest Boo-dist I've ever come across. Now just try to remain silent, meditate and live simply in the moment. Ohmm...

"Now in Chapter Two," Joe continued, not about to get off-topic, "*Divine Principle* teaches that Eve had sex with an angel. That's bizarre. You people actually believe in angels!"

There it is again, that contempt for religious concepts in general. Don't most *religions believe in angels?*

"In the book of Hebrews, the Bible says that angels are ministering spirits," I pointed out helpfully.

"I'm not into the *Old* Testament." Joe, in a bored tone, drew out the word "old" for emphasis.

Evidently, you're not into the New Testament either, or you would know that the book of Hebrews is a letter of St. Paul, you big dummy.

Trying hard not to show it, I inwardly celebrated my one-upmanship. Suddenly I was feeling less intimidated, for the moment.

After lunch, we were joined by Bridget, a former church member who had recently left after being kidnapped by her parents. John, Mary and Rosalind also came into the bedroom.

Bridget said, "I stopped believing in the *Divine Principle* when I realized the Historical Parallels weren't true. My faith had depended on that."

"Really?" I wondered out loud. "It's just history."

"Well," said Joe, "according to the Bible there were only 130 years of actual slavery in Egypt, not 400."

"But they were *in* Egypt for 400 years."

"Yes, Little Miss Arrogant, but they weren't *enslaved* for 400 years, yet the Divine Principle calls it the 400-year period of slavery. That's what I mean by a half-truth. And the Divided Kingdoms of East and West is called a 400-year period, but that can't be, because it's still going on now! Those two kingdoms never got back together."

"I think it just means that there were 400 years between the start of the division and the beginning of the captivity."

Joe was undaunted. "Alan Tate-Wood and Jane Williams made an extensive study of the Historical Parallels. They found that there were no consistent criteria for establishing the outer limits of each time period."

He produced a sheet of paper containing two color-coded diagrams. One represented the *Divine Principle* version of the historical periods, with one side neatly parallel to the other. In the second diagram, the colored boxes didn't match up quite as neatly.

But the periods are all there. All the colors are still there, in the right order.

Sue had told me long ago that there was a 2 to 3 percent margin of error concerning the lengths of the periods. I assumed that meant sometimes the numbers were rounded off.

"That just shows there's a three percent margin of error," I protested.

"What it shows, Little Miss Arrogant, is that the Divine Principle is fake!"

"Is not."

"Yes, it is! The historical parallels are just a fraudulent attempt to prove that the messiah should be born in 1920. They are simply the result of a warped mind, an obsessive, compulsive paranoid."

Oh God. Somehow, I have to give in to these people and pretend that they have broken my faith.

John said, "I've never even read the *Divine Principle*."

Oh my gosh, he is such an idiot.

Rosalind said, "I was disappointed that it wasn't unique. A lot of it was taken from other people's ideas. And I really didn't feel comfortable about the Fall of Man, especially the idea of Eve having sex with an angel."

There was my chance. I went for it.

"I had a hard time with that too," I admitted. It wasn't a lie. I was quite surprised when I first heard the teaching, and later questioned it, when studying it in more depth. But Sue had patiently explained that there were scriptural examples of angels having, or at least wanting to have, intercourse with humans (or vice-versa), like in Genesis 19 when two angels visited Lot in Sodom. Then there was Jude 6-7 which compared the sin of the angels to that of Sodom and Gomorrah.

But now was not the time for that. I needed to play dumb and weak, so I tried to act as if I was surrendering to my doubts.

"It *is* pretty bizarre," I went on and let out a long sigh as if I was on the verge of an existential crisis. "I somehow got sucked into it, though...oh my God, how could I have been so stupid?"

I tried to cry, and Rosalind came over and sat to the right of me on the bed. She patted me gently on the back. I kept my eyes down to hide my true feelings.

Joe and John exited the room, leaving the women behind to comfort me.

“It’s okay, we’ve all gone through this,” cooed Bridget. “It’s not your fault, your mind was controlled by the Moon cult.”

I felt an eye-roll coming on and fought to suppress it. Next thing I knew, my brother was in the room. He sat down on my left side and put his long arm around me. Neither of us knew what to say. I hadn’t seen my lovely brother in many years and he was tall, very tall, just like Joe had said.

But it was weird that he had his arm around me. We were never a “huggy” family. Had someone instructed him to do that? I wished we could be having this reunion under totally different circumstances.

Still, I was having my awaited “breakdown.” I had done my best. Would it be good enough?

We sat there in silence. It was an awkward, awkward moment.

11 - SNAPPING

The highest reach of injustice is to be deemed just when you are not.
—Plato.

Monday, August 8, 1983

It was Day Four, and something was off. I sensed, as I woke, an unusually heavy feeling which I could not identify. Was it despair? Danger? Impending doom? All three? Whatever it was, the heaviness pressed on my chest like hefty rocks.

I took a cold shower, which normally gave me a clear mind and a sense of having some control over my situation. Mary stayed with me in the bathroom, still betraying no emotion. She showed no open hostility but neither did she attempt to be friendly, which gave me a lonely feeling. Despite the refreshing shower, I could not shake off the cloud of gloom that seemed to surround me.

The events of the previous night had made me apprehensive. I had pretended to seriously question the *Divine Principle* and my involvement in the church and managed to squeeze out some fake tears. Some of the people acted happy and relieved, and I got to see my little brother, who wasn't little any more. I had faked my breakdown, but it felt awkward and strained.

Later I was allowed the rare privilege of leaving my cell to watch an old black and white movie on TV, *The Phantom of the Opera.* I loved the story. At the end, the phantom saves the life of the heroine, Christine, allowing a chandelier to fall on himself instead of her.

Sacrificial love! That's what makes good people good. Reverend Moon was right.

The movie was wonderful, but this morning I was on edge. It didn't help that I heard my mother's voice from somewhere in the house saying, "How do you like your eggs, Joe?" as though she were his personal servant.

I was right! She's been here the whole time, as I suspected. She's probably the chief cook for this whole crazy crew!

It annoyed me that she pandered to him like that, as though he deserved respect. It irked me that the deprogrammers were *working* for my family, most probably being paid a ridiculous amount of money to treat me like a piece of sub-human trash.

Sometimes life just wasn't fair. I remembered back to a time when I was fundraising in Melbourne in the 1970s and happened to go to a venue where people were gathered for horse races. Sometimes I did well at the races, especially major events like the Melbourne Cup. I walked into a racecourse bar to see if I could sell anything, and there he was: Father Lenny, sitting on a high stool at the bar with a beer in his hand and a cigarette resting on a nearby ashtray. We recognized each other immediately; he was the uncle of an old friend of mine from primary school. I'll never forget the look of sheer contempt on his face as he said the words that crushed and humiliated me.

"What would your mother say if she could see you now?"

I turned and left the bar. The shock of the encounter had left me speechless, otherwise I might have said what was on *my* mind:

Well, what would your *mother say if she could see* you *now? A holy priest drinking, smoking and betting on the horses?*

But as soon as I thought the words, I knew how pointless they would have been. The cruel irony was that Father Lenny's mother would still be proud of him, because it was okay for Catholic priests to smoke, drink and gamble; but it was not okay for young women to participate in new religious movements, even if their lifestyle was purer than Antarctic snow. I felt the sting of injustice.

Besides, why did he have to be so mean? Weren't priests supposed to be kind and loving, like Jesus?

A similar double standard was apparent in the present moment. The faith-breakers were not good people! They were bad people pretending to be good; but why couldn't anybody else see that?

Somehow it was okay for my mother to kowtow to these convicted felons, treat them like kings and pay them Lord knows how much money while holding me, her own daughter, against my will in a dingy little room with people harassing and ridiculing me and my religion from morning to night. Life wasn't fair.

She never even asked how I liked *my* eggs!

Things got steadily worse as Joe Junior arrived in the bedroom just as I was starting to eat something.

He was obviously in a bad mood and started yelling right away.

"Why does Moon put so much emphasis on making money? Jesus didn't do that. Neither did Buddha. It's for his own personal gain, his own personal power!"

Oh, dear God. I had the sudden urge to charge at him with my plastic fork but managed to restrain myself.

That's when I knew that I'd failed. My prepared breakdown had not been convincing. The others might have been fooled by it, but not Joe Junior. He was a *professional* who knew a genuine breakdown when he saw one.

I was in deep trouble. I was up the proverbial creek without a back-up plan, and now, by the tone of his voice I could tell he was turning *up* the pressure rather than turning it down as I had hoped might happen today.

"What if Moon told you to kill your father?" he demanded to know. "Would you do it?"

"Of course not!"

"But Moon is the messiah and you obey everything he says!"

"But he would never tell me to kill my father!"

"But what if he did?"

Then I said something that my family would hold against me for years to come. I said, flippantly, "Well, my father has to die sometime anyway..."

I still don't know why I said it. I never had a desire to kill my father. But Joe was so insistent, I had to answer his inane question one way or the other.

"So, you would *kill* your own father!" Joe yelled.

"No!"

"But that's what you just said! 'Well, my father has to die sometime anyway,' right? I just heard you say that."

"It's a completely stupid question to begin with. What do you expect? Stop asking stupid questions!"

"You are one arrogant *bitch*," snarled Joe.

The word stung me like a slap. Normally nobody spoke to me like that, not even mean people that I'd met while witnessing or fund-raising. One time a person had flicked cigarette ash on my arm while I was street witnessing in Adelaide, but this was worse. It was unjust, hurtful and demeaning. Theoretically I believed in loving one's enemy, but at that moment I hated Joe Alexander and his entourage, including my mother, with a fierce passion. I could feel something rising inside me, a dangerous cocktail of panic, laced with resentment and indignation.

I had run out of tactics. If I ignored them, they accused me of non-thinking. If I engaged in argument, I was an arrogant, smart-ass bitch. If I pretended to succumb to their badgering, my limited acting skills betrayed me. Now Joe was getting impatient and the pressure was intense. He thought he could break my spirit, but he was frustrated because I hadn't truly "snapped" yet, like I was supposed to.

I didn't know how much more pressure I could take. There had been moments when I felt something starting to unravel inside me, when I started doubting myself and asking the unthinkable questions: *What if all these people are right, and I'm wrong? What if I should have trusted my parents all along? What about the PR sisters, the second wife, the bigamy, the manufacturing of weapons?* I desperately needed answers.

If I caved in to self-doubt, how could I ever trust myself again? How would I ever believe in anything again? A major problem with deprogramming was that they would rip my faith out of me without giving me anything to replace it. They would leave me incomplete like an amputee. I couldn't let that happen.

I shouldn't even be in this situation in the first place. If I made a mistake joining the Unification Church, I can figure that out by myself. It's not their job to tell me what to think or with whom to associate! They have no right to keep me here against my will. Don't I have any rights? How dare they keep me in this room like a prisoner! It's not right. They should let me go...

Then the dam burst. I really did snap, just not in the way they wanted me to. I came emotionally unstuck and somehow forced my way past Joe and out into the hallway, screaming, crying and shrieking at the top of my shaky voice.

"You can't do this to me! It's not fair! I can't even get out of this house! You have no right to keep me here! I hate you. I hate all of you!"

I could see my mother standing in the hallway. The hysteria must have caught her attention. I still remember her frowning face which looked disappointed, ashamed, angry. *Oh, my crazy brainwashed daughter is throwing a tantrum. How embarrassing.*

Someone forced me back into the bedroom and I lay face-down on the bed, sobbing, no longer able or even caring to contain the tears of frustration and the flood of impotent rage.

12 - BLUE BABY

Faith is not the clinging to a shrine but an endless pilgrimage of the heart.
—Abraham Joshua Heschel

As the heaving sobs eventually started to subside, I had a vague sense of deja-vu, of having experienced this scenario, or something like it, before. The feeling hovered at the periphery of my consciousness like a blurry and distant echo from the past. Then it suddenly came into focus.

I remembered lying in a different bedroom, down a different hallway in Dunedin, 1976. Another tall, lean man had been harassing me. It was my flatmate, Marty. He'd been so unfair, so unkind! He'd even tried to follow me to my room, but I'd locked him out. What had led up to that? I recalled the events of that day and the days prior to it. It was when my little sister died.

I lived in a cheap, cinder-block flat near the university. It wasn't pretty, but it was convenient, affordable and I loved having my own room, after always sharing with a roommate at Dominican Hall and before that, my sisters. Christine, my older sister, now lived on the hillside in an older, nicer flat that had a telephone. She was the one who got the call from home and came to relay the message. It was June, and bitter cold. She knocked on the door of my tiny bedroom where I was studying with an electric heater on. Her expression was unusually serious.

"Genie died last night."

"What? Genie can't die."

She explained that a bad flu was going around, and Genie's heart was too weak. We cried together. Then we had to make plans to go home for the rosary and funeral. Practical preparations like having to walk downtown and buy train tickets for the two of us gave me something to focus on. Half in a daze, I walked down George Street, where I happened to pass Ian, the headmaster of CCD, which was Sunday School for Catholic children. I was one of his volunteer teachers. "I won't be able to do CCD this Sunday," I explained. "My sister died, and I'll be in Invercargill for the weekend."

"That's very unfortunate. My sympathy." Ian was so nice and sincere, and he always knew the right thing to say. At 22, he seemed so grown up. At 18, I was trying to be grown-up, but sometimes still felt like a child.

We went home on the *Southerner Express*. I looked out the train windows at the late afternoon winter sunlight illuminating bright yellow broom bushes and gorse bushes which sped by us as we chugged through the countryside. Memories of little Genie came flooding to my mind. She was a "blue baby," born with a hole in her heart, which was considered inoperable at that time. She was also afflicted with Downs Syndrome. My parents were shocked to know they had a "Mongol baby," a common description in the 1960s, but they determined to keep the child and love her like their others. They explained to us five older siblings that Genie would be "intellectually handicapped" and might never develop academically or socially. However, we must love her and treat her the same as we would if she were perfectly normal. This proved to be an easy thing, since Genie had the sweetest nature and was the most lovable out of our whole family. She adored people. Whenever I came home from school for a visit, she would welcome me at the glass sliding door with a huge smile. "You *been*!" She might never learn to read or write, but whatever Genie lacked in intellect, she more than made up for in heart.

By the mid-1970s, my parents had replaced their old house with a new one, built by my father's own hands in his spare time. Mum now enjoyed an electric range and central heating. No more coal deliveries, no more frigid mornings. Life was easier now, but losing Genie was devastating for them, and for all of us. We tried to be strong and brave.

"Let's sit together, for the rosary," said Anne, my younger sister. We were so close in age we'd grown up like best friends.

"Okay. I won't cry."

"Me either."

So, we sat together, to be strong and brave, but failed miserably. Either Anne, or someone else, let out a sob, which then triggered an avalanche. I cried, Anne cried, and we just seemed to keep setting each other off. At the height of our emotional release, I cried so hard that I lost control of my bladder. I continued to weep helplessly as the warm moisture slowly spread through several layers of my winter clothing.

After the rosary, Anne and I met Eileen and Therese in the church foyer. They were Mum's cousins and our first cousins once removed. Devout Catholics, they were kind, gentle, middle-aged spinsters who had taken care of their elderly parents until their death, then just stayed together. Taking one look at our pink, tear-stained faces Eileen and Therese were moved with compassion. They took our hands and rubbed them. "You poor things!" they said.

Neighbors, friends, and relatives crowded into the parish church for the funeral and into our house for the reception afterward. They brought soups, casseroles, breads, cakes, biscuits and every kind of comfort food imaginable. I ate a lot. I ate far too much and felt ill afterward. It was a distressing time.

My uncle drove my sister and me back to Dunedin on Sunday evening. During the two-hour drive, I thought back to one day, a few days earlier, when my Dad asked who wanted to go to the funeral home for the "viewing." I jumped at the opportunity, having never seen a dead body before, and wanting to see my sister one last time. But it didn't look like her. It was her body, yet the essence of her was gone. It was like looking at the empty shell of something. I had the sense, and the conviction, that the real Genie was elsewhere. She must be in heaven, with Jesus. I pictured her on Jesus' lap, and him bouncing her on his knee. *Genie must be in a good place*. I felt at peace. As if to seal my peace, the evening sky had become beautiful like an artist's watercolor, awash with pale pinks and blues.

Baby pink, baby blue.

By the time I got back to my flat I was calm, dry-eyed and ready to dive back into my student life. Except for Marty, who was in a dark mood.

"You didn't even love your sister." He tilted his head proudly, looking down at me.

"What? I did so."

"No, you didn't love her, because she was handicapped." From the way he slurred his words I could tell he'd been drinking.

"I did so love her!"

"No, you didn't. If you loved her, you'd be more upset. Look at you, you're happy, not even grieving."

"I'm happy because she's in heaven with Jesus!"

I started down the hallway toward my room, feeling myself start to cry at the sheer injustice of his comments. I didn't want to hear anymore. He followed me.

"You just couldn't love her because she was handicapped. You're probably *relieved* now that she's dead," he taunted.

Unbelievable! I shut the door before he could come into my room, which seemed to be his intention. I locked it and lay on the bed.

Knock, knock! Knock, knock!

Go away! Go away! I hope he doesn't break the door down!

Knock, knock!

Finally, it stopped, and I lay there in shock, my heart pounding.

That was only the beginning of my troubles with Marty and the flatmates. It turned out to be a turbulent year in which my child-like faith in Jesus and the Catholic Church came under an onslaught of tests and trials. But at least, during those struggles, I had the freedom to come and go. I could tell my troubles to trusted friends like Celine and others. I could talk to my uncle, who was a priest. I could go home and talk to my mother, who said, "Don't compromise!" It was good advice, which I had not forgotten. I was outnumbered in my student flat by non-believers, four to one. But at least, I could get away. And in the case of Marty, I could lock him out.

But here, they had me, locked *in*.

Poem for Genevieve

Evening sky was double hue,
Baby pink and baby blue.
She was a "blue baby," yes -
blue baby girl in a pink dress.
Loved everyone she met,
heart as big as a Jumbo Jet.
How weak that heart was no one knew,
until that June she caught the flu.
At the rosary we cried and cried,
couldn't believe our Genie* had died.
An uncle drove my sister and me
back home. We sat quietly.
The twilight sky, double hue
was baby pink and baby blue.

—Maree Gauper, January 18, 2018
***Pronounced Jenny**

13 - A PILGRIM'S PROGRESS

How could we have discovered great lands, if we dare not travel?
—Lailah Gifty Akita

1975

The look on Sister Bernadette's face was unforgettable. She was wearing a little white nightcap, tied under her chin with narrow ribbons, and her deeply-lined middle-aged face registered shock, horror, puzzlement, perhaps a little terror. What is this girl doing at the top of the fire escape, knocking on my bedroom window?

I didn't know what else to do. I had been up early Sunday morning, when the rest of the Dominican Hall of Residence was sleeping, to prepare for my CCD class. Someone would be picking me up at 8am. I was running a hot bath to thaw out my skin and bones from the chilly Dunedin weather. I'd left items of clothing on the clothesline overnight, and went outside to get them, leaving the bathwater running. I'd forgotten that the front door automatically locked behind you, unless you made sure to move the latch so that it wouldn't. *I locked myself out.* I checked the other doors. All locked. My bathwater was running and would surely overflow if someone didn't turn it off. What could I do?

The nuns slept upstairs. I could see the little windows of their rooms which, in a different era, were probably servants' quarters of a wealthy household. A fire escape ladder rose from the ground up to one of those windows. I had to take it; there was no other option, mortifying as it seemed. Tap! Knock! Knock! *Please somebody, wake up!*

Sister Bernadette saved the day and turned off the bathwater. She seemed irritated. I felt embarrassed both by my careless mistake in getting locked out, and by having to knock on a sleeping nun's window, from the top of a fire escape!

Another time, for a prank, some girls had strung items of someone's clothing and bed linens across the balcony outside my room, on the side of the house which faced the road and neighborhood. Our entire floor got the blame, and Sister Bernadette was irate.

"Take those down at once! We are not a third-rate boarding house!"

I began to think seriously about the following year. Unlike some of my Dom Hall friends, I would not plan on a second year there. I would move out and get a flat of my own. I felt confined, restricted.

For one thing, Dominican Hall had so many rules:

Residents must be in no later than 11:00 pm.

No male visitors will be permitted beyond the communal area.

Residents must arrive for meals in a timely manner, etc. etc.

Since the age of four, I had been scolded and controlled by nuns. Even if some of them were rather lovely, I was tired of it. I wanted out. Fortunately, Diane, a good friend since high school, felt the same.

***

1976

I wanted a "mixed flat" with men and women. This had become an accepted practice in the 1970s. My strict parents were alarmed. Sex before marriage was a mortal sin.

"Mixed flatting? You'd be living with strange men. You could end up pregnant!" wrote my mother.

"Don't worry," I wrote back. "I haven't gone off the deep end. Anyway, there's an unwritten rule that flatmates don't get romantically involved with each other." They calmed down.

It was exhilarating when Diane and I finally found our new home, a basic, cinderblock, rectangular building with five small bedrooms and a common area for cooking, eating and socializing. The plainness of it was irrelevant to me, I was so intoxicated by my new freedom. The day we moved in, I walked the short distance to the downtown shops and purchased a small electric heater and a bright orange sheepskin rug that would go perfectly with my orange bedspread. I also signed up for Weight Watchers, now that I could buy my own food and plan my own meals. I would lose weight! Maybe attract a boyfriend! The new school year seemed full of possibilities.

During the first term, various flatmates came and went. By the second term we had five settled occupants: Diane and I, plus Richard, a medical student from Christchurch; Marty, also a medical student, from Wellington, and Nick, a part-time student from rural Rangiora. At first, Marty was perfectly nice and we all got along. Richard, the natural leader of the group, collected our rent and electricity money to pay the landlord who stopped by each week. He also had us put money in a "kitty" for groceries and gave each person a weekday night for cooking. My day was Thursday. On weekends you were on your own.

I had an odd, mismatched assortment of hopes and dreams. On the one hand, I aspired to someday marry a doctor and live in an expensive suburb of Christchurch, like Fendalton, where Richard was from. I would raise a family and dabble in music and art in my spare time; I would rise above my working-class roots. It helped that there was a continuous stream of medical students dropping in and out of our flat, friends of Richard and Marty. Medical School in Dunedin was the hardest school to get into. Those who made it, knew they were a special group, the crème de la crème. They were delightfully witty and charmingly arrogant. I was particularly attracted to Pete, one of Richard's classmates who also happened to be an accomplished cello player. Perhaps he would notice me after I lost my excess weight...

On the other hand, I admired women who were independently successful, especially in the arts. I read about New Zealanders like short-story writer Katharine Mansfield and landscape artist, Frances Hodgkins. Both women left New Zealand and spent most of their working lives overseas. To be like them, I would need to travel. When a friend invited me and Diane to go to Australia for the summer holidays, we accepted. It seemed like destiny.

I continued to love Jesus and my Catholic faith, but I also yearned to be more like Jocelyn. Tall, winsome Jocelyn was a fellow student from some of my Music II classes, including History of Opera. Usually in music, I sat with my Catholic friend, Maria, from Timaru. Both of us noticed Jocelyn, who stood out from the rest of the class. She was older than most of us, being in her mid-twenties (we guessed). Jocelyn had her own style, like a character from a children's storybook. Whereas the general student body dressed in practical, conservative clothing, Jocelyn had a Bohemian flair, with her long velvet dresses and her thick chestnut hair, all plaited and tied with velvet ribbons. Maria and I were in awe of her, and so it was extremely thrilling that she invited us to her house one night to have dinner and study *The Marriage of Figaro.*

Jocelyn lived with her parents in a lovely house on a hill. Before dinner, while listening to Rachmaninov records, we learned more about her life.

"When I was a teenager, I ran away from home and lived in the mountains. Then I fell in love with a man. After five years with him, the love turned to hatred and he turned to drugs."

How tragic! I wasn't sure which was more dramatic—Jocelyn's story-telling, or the 2nd Rachmaninov Piano Concerto which provided the soundtrack. In any case, the combination was thrilling. "But now I have a new boyfriend, who lives in Waitati," she finished, as the music calmed down.

Maria shared with us some of her past crushes. I lamented about Pete the cello player.

"I sit there in orchestra, admiring his lovely *vibrato*. Especially in the Mendelssohn Concerto, where the two leading cellists do this exquisite counterpoint passage with the First Violins. But he doesn't even know my name. It's hopeless!" I pouted. Fortunately, Jocelyn understood hopelessness.

"Oh, don't worry. Earlier this year I was in love with Professor Drummond! His translation of *Orfeo* is absolutely marvelous."

Maria and I giggled at the thought of Jocelyn having a crush on our opera teacher. Then I shared some more.

"When I was in high school, I wasn't allowed to have crushes. One time, we were watching *Gidget* on TV, and Gidget's friend had a huge crush on some boy. Mum was watching this show while doing the ironing or something, and she said, 'Don't *you* go having crushes on boys.' But I can't help it."

Jocelyn was sympathetic. "Of course, it's only natural."

***

It was around mid-year that things changed. It started with the nasty incident with Marty, when he accused me of not loving my sister, and tried to follow me to my room. I told my Catholic friends about it at the Victorian dinner party which Maria and I hosted for Paul and David, my old friends from Invercargill, one weekend when all the flatmates were away. I made Beef Stroganoff and decorated the table with a white cloth, yellow napkins, candles and fresh daffodils. We rented black dresses and frilly white aprons and pretended we were Victorian maids. My dress was a whole size smaller than I usually wore, but it fit, like a glove. I'd lost a lot of weight, which felt wonderful.

"I was quite scared of Marty that night," I explained. Paul was instantly sympathetic. He had a good heart.

"That was really horrible what he did to you."

"Yes, and that's not all. He has sleepovers twice a week with Joanne, and on in-between nights, he's with Jan, who's Joanne's best friend, and neither of them seems to realize it." Maria's eyes widened, and her jaw dropped slightly.

"So...he's a bully *and* a two-timer. That *is* horrible."

"We should try and get a flat together next year," suggested David. "You don't need to deal with all this crap."

"Yes, that would be much nicer," I agreed, and then we played piano, waltzed and sang choruses from *Orfeo* until 2am.

***

One evening in my flat, we were all doing the dishes together. Diane, who was attending Teachers' College while also taking Psychology Intermediate, by mid-year had serious doubts about her faith. "I don't see what's wrong with the pill! My Mum's on the pill, my sister too. Why does the Pope have to make such a big deal out of it?" She scrubbed a pot a little too energetically.

"He no play-a the game, he no make-a the rules!" Nick chimed in, grinning broadly, while depositing silverware into a drawer.

"But he does make the rules," I pointed out.

Richard added his opinion. "Realistically, unless you want millions of unwanted pregnancies, it's a workable solution." With a toss of his head, he flipped a shaggy forelock out of his eyes. "After all, 75 percent of unmarried women under 25 'do it'."

The statistic was shocking, and I felt personally offended by it. "I'm glad to be in the minority."

"You mean, you don't believe in sex outside of marriage?" Richard wondered.

"No, I don't."

"Shit!" said Nick, in a high-pitched voice, obviously taken aback. Richard dropped a dishtowel and stared at me with his mouth open. The tension was escalating and I could feel my heart pounding with anxiety.

"So, what's the reasoning behind the strict Catholic teaching on contraception?" asked Nick. He sounded genuinely curious, so I tried to formulate a thoughtful response.

"Sex is designed for pleasure but also for procreation. It should be limited to exclusive and permanent relationships, such as marriage. Married couples don't even really need the pill, since there are other, more natural means of family planning."

Diane was visibly upset. She looked up from the sink and our eyes met. "You're just quoting from the catechism, because that's what you've been *conditioned* to do! You don't question anything. You need to open your mind! Stop being so self-righteous."

"I'm not self-righteous, I'm right!"

Fortunately, I had a Weight Watchers meeting to attend, which provided a perfect excuse to leave the flat and get away for a while. I felt dejected and alone, like the Christian character in *A Pilgrim's Progress*, trudging through the Slough of Despond.

***

Sunday nights at the flat became a battleground. We would sit at the table having philosophical discussions about the future: clones, nuclear power, destiny and the existence of God. Determined not to compromise, I openly proclaimed my firm belief in God, Jesus and an afterlife. Nick was nice about it. He had a history of depression and was on medication, which gave him a certain vulnerability and humility the others lacked. "I admire your faith and the stability it gives you. Personally, I feel God is a figment of the imagination, but I do respect your position."

"I think religion is just a way for people to make sense out of life," said Diane, "but there's no absolute truth."

Richard, generally kind and good-humored, was also an atheist. One Sunday night he was more abrasive than usual. "Faith is just the result of conditioning. Anyone who's done Psych Intermediate knows that. You're only Catholic because you were born into it. If you'd been born in Indonesia, you'd be a Moslem. We're merely a product of our experiences."

Not to be outdone, Marty chimed in, chuckling a little. "Yes, you could try being a little less fanatical. It's pretty fuck-witted to be that fanatical."

My legs had turned to jelly, and I could feel my chin and lower lip twitching and wobbling. I had no idea how to respond. I went to my room. That night I wrote in my diary:

I was so angry, I cleaned my whole room and beat hell out of my sheepskin rug.

***

The next night I told my good friend Celine everything. We were both English Honors students and sometimes studied Chaucer together. I poured out my troubles, as we walked round and round the outside of the university library. She reassured me that faith was something real. "You can count on my moral support at any time." Celine was a rock, a true and loyal friend. On the way home, I treated myself to a large bottle of Slimline Diet Orangeade from the corner store and went to bed in a more optimistic mood.

***

Marty was relentless. His attacks were not limited to Sunday evening table discussions. One evening as I was leaving the flat to attend Mass, he sneered at me. "It's just self-hypnosis!" Another day, as I diligently weighed food on my Weight Watchers scale, he taunted me in a voice dripping with condescension: "Stick to the *rules!!*"

Later that day I wrote in my journal:

Marty and Richard think they know everything. Marty really doesn't like me at the moment. Thinks I'm a fanatical fuckwit. 'Stick to the rules,' he said, scathingly. But the rules work, and HE's the fuckwit. I lost 1.4 kilograms last week!

One night I tried to be a peacemaker and made scones and baked beans for the whole flat. I knocked on Marty's door to let him know.

"No need to knock, it's not a bloody *priory*," he snarled.

***

Celine was marvelous, but I needed other rocks of additional support to keep myself from getting stuck in the Slough of Despond. I purchased a book, *Jesus Rediscovered*, by Malcolm Muggeridge, British journalist and recent convert to Christianity, who was credited with bringing Mother Theresa to popular attention in the west. I also had an opportunity to hear him speak over the radio. Moved and empowered by his words, I wrote in my journal:

He leadeth me beside still waters. He restoreth my soul.

FANTASTIC radio talk by Malcolm Muggeridge (my hero!) He never needed a God—God wanted him! He felt like Francis Thompson in The Hound of Heaven and is now waiting for the final spring of the hound. He sees Time as fantasy, Eternity as reality. Power as fantasy, Love as reality; the Incarnation as a point where Eternity and Time intersected, forming a cross.

***

I fully expected Ian to be one of my allies in this spiritual warfare. After all, he was the CCD headmaster and obviously a good person of deep faith. At 22, he was a well-built and attractive young man, with the classic Celtic coloring of dark hair and blue eyes. One Saturday night he came to my flat, to let me know there would be no CCD classes the next day. We talked from after dinner until 10:30pm. I explained to him some of the challenges I'd been facing, and his responses shocked me. In my diary I described him as "surprisingly unorthodox, liberal, free-thinking, un-Biblical and very influenced by Intermediate Psychology." At one point he stated, "The crucifixion and resurrection are really quite irrelevant," so super-casually, that I could've burst into tears of disappointment. In some ways his flippant rationalizations were more devastating to my already shaky confidence than any of Marty's atheistic onslaughts.

I felt this was the Valley of the Shadow of Death. It was the hardest thing to endure, that someone whose faith and character I so highly respected had a God and a religion that were so vastly different from my own. Yet we were part of the same church; we taught the same group of children! I felt for a while that I was in the pits of darkness, unable to see my way ahead.

I listened to more Muggeridge, which helped. He said, "Christian clergy are hypocritical and corrupt and church-going is being phased out."

Yet, God is not being phased out.

Muggeridge was a different kind of Christian than those I'd been exposed to in the past. So was Ian. Yet they were both men of good character who loved God. I still considered Ian a friend even though his opinions caused me to struggle mightily. In the long run, he helped me open my mind to realize that there are many ways of understanding God and Jesus, and that I needed to be willing to examine them.

***

I continued to lose weight on the Weight Watchers plan. Pete, the cello-playing medical student, never noticed me. Eventually I worked up the courage to ask him out, but he said "No". One time, Ian asked me out and I said "Yes". We had a lovely time at the

Dunedin Rugby Club. He took me home in a taxi and gave me a kiss on the cheek. I floated into my flat on a cloud.

As the school year was winding down, Maria and Jocelyn came for dinner. Jocelyn was wearing a clingy velvet dress under a fur coat and an ostrich-feather stole. "What have you been up to lately?" I asked her.

"I've been hanging out with *insane* poets at the Captain Cook. I've been teaching juvenile delinquents at Abbotsford. I vomited out of sheer nerves before one of my final exams and I recently told my Waitati boyfriend he could stick his relationship up his bum!" We all laughed.

Then she told us about her friend Malcolm who'd changed his last name to Gramophone, and who once tried to blow up the fertilizer works.

No one had more interesting friends or did more exciting and romantic things than Jocelyn. I would never be as exciting as her. Yet I admired her beauty and originality, her confidence and self-assurance. *She's a free spirit. That's what I want to be.*

1976 had been a wild roller-coaster ride, during which I collided head-on with 1970s popular culture. It left me primed for the next stage of the journey: Australia.

14 - "THE GAME IS AFOOT!"

To win the fight you've got to have the right strategy and the right resources, because victories don't come by accident.
—The War Room (movie)

August 4, 1983

Until the phone call, it was an ordinary Thursday evening at 24 St. Stephens Avenue, the elegant two-storied home that reputedly once belonged to the Queen of Tonga, but which now housed the headquarters of the Unification Church of New Zealand.

The telephone rang at about 11:00pm. Pam, a petite woman with long auburn hair, was upstairs making sure the kitchen was ship shape before heading off to bed. She picked up the phone extension in the hallway just outside the kitchen.

The caller did not identify himself, which was odd to begin with.

He said, "Maree has decided she's not coming back for a few days. She's going to stay with us, possibly for a week or more."

"Us?" asked Pam. "Who are the 'us'?" but the mystery caller had already hung up.

"Very strange," Pam murmured.

Sarah came upstairs only moments afterward. An Australian in her late twenties who had been appointed National Leader of the New Zealand church in 1982, she was tall, lean, energetic and empathic. She took her responsibilities seriously which included acting as spiritual advisor to this small group of young people.

Pam told Sarah about the call, reporting each word as accurately as she could.

"I agree, that is strange. Disturbing, too. Let's talk about it with Chris when he gets back."

Chris was Public Affairs officer for the National Headquarters. He was 29 and had been a member for five years after meeting the Unification Church while traveling in Europe. He had a Teacher's College diploma and was working on a bachelor's degree at Auckland University. That night he had stayed late at the university library to study and it was just after 11:00 pm when he arrived back at the church center.

"What's going on?" he asked, seeing Sarah and Pam in the upstairs hallway and immediately sensing the tense atmosphere.

"Maree went out with friends and didn't come back," said Sarah.

"That's unusual." Chris's inquisitive mind already began to analyze the information.

"Yes, and there was this strange phone call from somebody saying she'd be gone for a while, like a week or more."

"Odd," said Chris. He had a bad feeling.

Ever since the deprogramming movement had gathered momentum in the United States, Chris had taken an academic as well as personal interest in it. As a part of his degree work, he had taken a class in the Sociology of Religion. He had studied the phenomenon of deprogramming and the Anti-Cult Movement in some depth with a Scientologist friend who was a recognized expert. He kept in regular contact with the legal department of the Unification Church's American headquarters in New York City.

He was keenly aware that the despicable practice was not confined to the United States. He knew of several New Zealanders who had joined the movement elsewhere but found themselves in an abduction-like situation while at home visiting their parents. Bridget Gardner left the church after her encounter with American deprogrammers; yet she reached out and maintained a cordial relationship with the members in Auckland. One month ago, Rosalind Menzies had been involved in a deprogramming event locally. Because the danger was looming close to home, Chris tried to be aware of each member's situation, especially the attitude of their family towards the church.

"Maree's family aren't the sort to go Bolshie...she has regular communication with them and they saw each other not that long ago," Chris recalled, referring to Maree's parents' visit to Melbourne in July 1982 which had reportedly been cordial.

"Traditional Irish Catholic families, like mine for example, are not usually troublesome. There's trust between parents and children. Maree's an intelligent woman who's very much her own person. I'm sure she'll be fine," continued Chris, trying to reassure himself as well as the others.

"I don't have a good feeling about this," said Margaret, a dark-haired woman with thick eyeglasses, who had just joined them.

"Shouldn't we go to the police?" asked Pam.

"I don't know...do we have the address of that place she was going? What's the name of that friend of hers, David isn't it?" asked Chris. "She might still be there."

"I have it somewhere," Sarah remembered. "We went there once, together."

Shortly afterward, Sarah and Chris were on David's front doorstep. Chris pounded on the door, which was opened by a surprised occupant.

"Where is she?" Chris demanded.

"I don't know. She's not here," said David, trembling slightly. "You can come in and look around if you want."

"Tell us what happened. She came here for dinner and then what?"

"No, she was never here for dinner. She wasn't here at all." His voice was shaky.

"So where was the dinner party?"

"There was no dinner party. I didn't even see her, and I don't know where she is. She's gone with her mother somewhere."

As they drove back up Parnell Rise, Chris, gripping the steering wheel tightly, reflected on the visit.

"David was telling the truth."

"I agree."

"I thought he was going to pee himself! His nervousness means that he knows something."

"But perhaps not enough to be able to give anything away," Sarah finished the thought.

"My gut tells me something is seriously awry. Bridget Gardner's parents hired American faith-breakers and hid Bridget at their lake house in Taupo. What if something like that happened to Maree?"

"It's possible."

Chris took a left turn at the top of the rise, where the Anglican Cathedral dominated a hilltop corner. They were almost home.

"Why don't you take a rest while I go to the Police Station?"

Chris conceded.

***

It was close to midnight when Sarah and Pam arrived at the Auckland Central Police Station and explained their predicament to Detective Inspector Hugglestone.

"There's nothing we can do," he said dismissively. "Our office hours are over for the day. You'll have to come back in the morning and make a formal complaint."

"But we're concerned that this woman may have been kidnapped by her family," Pam insisted, "and they may be forcing her to change her beliefs."

"I'm sure there's nothing to worry about. She'll show up when she wants to." He exhaled, leaned his forearms on the counter between them and tapped a ballpoint pen on its cold surface.

"But what if she doesn't?"

Hugglestone smiled and looked Pam in the eye.

"Well then, you will have lost another disciple, won't you? Not much I can do about that."

***

"I can't believe how horrible that policeman was," said Pam, in the car as they drove back to Parnell. "I thought the police were supposed to help people and protect them, but he seemed *happy* that one of our members is missing. He was really, really rude."

"Yes, it's disheartening. I just want to go to the prayer room and ask for some direction. Everything feels so confusing right now."

***

Friday August 5, 1:30 am

Ralph had an extension phone beside his bed and picked it up as soon as it started ringing. He answered cheerfully.

"Ralph speaking."

Ralph's son Warren lived with him in the suburb of Mount Albert. Warren was a Licensed Aircraft Maintenance Engineer for Air New Zealand. Blessed with a keen mechanical mind and a meticulous eye for details, he was good at his job. A phone call from work in the middle of the night was not unusual. If an aircraft had an unexpected problem or if staff were needed to go overseas or come to work at a different time than usual, Air New Zealand might call any time of the day or night.

But this time it wasn't work calling. "It's Sarah from the church," Ralph informed Warren a few seconds after answering the phone.

Warren had met the Unification Church while on a visit to California with his job. He later visited the Auckland center and gradually became involved, attending Sunday Services and helping maintain the church's small fleet of vehicles. If needed, he was happy to lend one of his own vehicles for the church members' use. He had never lived in the church center himself, preferring to keep his job and stay with his elderly widowed father.

Warren got up quickly and picked up the telephone in the dining room. For Sarah to be calling at this time of night, it had to be something serious.

"Hello?"

"Maree's been kidnapped," she said, "and the car won't start. Can we borrow yours?"

Maree, kidnapped?

"Sure." Warren hung up and got ready to leave as fast as he could.

Warren was a spiritually sensitive person whom some might call a psychic. While driving to Parnell he tried to tune in to the shocking situation.

"Where are you?" he asked urgently. Then thinking it might help to be more specific while asking questions of the cosmos he called out, "Where is Maree? Where is Maree Ryan?" using the maiden name of the young woman he had come to think of as a sister.

A word came to him that sounded like Whangarei.

"Whangarei?" He asked.

"No. Whangaparaoa," came the reply.

***

Meanwhile Sarah, having prayed for guidance, was being led intuitively to Bridget Gardner. Bridget was the key, somehow. But how? She thought about the lake house in Taupo. What if Maree's parents, in collusion with Bridget's, had taken Maree there? This hunch agreeing with Chris's suspicions, they decided to go immediately to Taupo, except that the car would not start. Thank goodness for Warren.

As Sarah, Chris and Grant, a new member still in his teens, took Warren back to his house, they explained why they were heading to Taupo, even though it was 170 miles away, a three-hour drive. Warren openly supported the plan while privately questioning it.

Sarah's going south. Shouldn't she be going north?

Rather than presenting a case for his own preference, which would involve heading north to Whangaparaoa, Warren decided to save that for later. Sarah had obviously set her mind on Taupo and sensing her fierce determination, Warren guessed this would not be a good time for discussion or argument. He would defer to her judgment for now and went back to bed.

The other three drove through the night with Chris mostly resting in the back seat after his long day at school. Sarah and Grant were wide awake, fueled by adrenaline and a sense of outrage. Finally, they reached Taupo and located the cabin.

"This is it," said Grant. "No lights on, but it *is* late. They could be sleeping."

"Any vehicles?" asked Chris, rubbing his eyes and pushing himself into a sitting position.

Sarah scanned the property, noting the empty driveway. "I don't see any vehicles. Looks deserted."

It had evidently been a wasted trip.

***

It was morning by the time they arrived back in Auckland. Sarah and Grant took a much-needed rest while Chris decided to call his friend Mike Ferris at Scientology and bring him up to speed. Scientologists were well-versed in the history and tactics of the Anti-Cult Movement. Even though at this point no one knew if deprogrammers were involved, it was a possibility they would need to consider. Mike agreed to come over the next day and talk over the case with Chris.

Chris got himself toast and tea and sat down in the church office downstairs. He needed time to be alone, to think. Something big and probably bad was going on. He was determined to get to the bottom of it.

Who would know something? Who might be in on it? Her family in Invercargill, of course! And the uncle, in Grey Lynn.

Chris's sharp features brightened. His cool blue eyes lit up at the thought of interviewing them. He chuckled to himself.

"The game is afoot!" he said out loud, quoting Sherlock Holmes. He would phone them as soon as he finished eating.

His first call was to the Ryan household in Invercargill. An older male voice answered, whom Chris assumed to be Maree's father.

"Hi! This is Chris Newman from the Unification Church."

"We know who you are," said the voice, cautiously.

"We're wondering about Maree's whereabouts," Chris went on. "We haven't seen her since late yesterday afternoon, so we're quite concerned."

"Well we're not concerned and anyhow, it's none of your business."

"I disagree. She's an important part of our community and we'd like to know where she is. Actually, we're about to report her to the police as a missing person," Chris announced brightly.

"She's not missing. She's all right."

"But how would you know that?" Chris persisted.

"That's no concern of yours. It's not your worry."

"Well, where is she then, since you seem to know so much about it?"

"You don't need to know. The main thing is, she's all right."

"But how do you know that?"

"We just do."

Chris ended the call and tried to figure out what to make of it. Maree's father was completely nonchalant and unconcerned about his daughter's disappearance. Apparently, he knew something but wasn't inclined to share details.

His daughter's gone missing and he's not even worried? He's in on it. They've taken her and hidden her somewhere.

Next on the list was Nick Maloney, Maree's middle-aged bachelor uncle, a former Marist brother who taught mathematics in Ponsonby.

"Nick here," answered a voice.

After some brief formalities, Chris got straight to the point. "We're afraid your niece may have been kidnapped. She's been missing since yesterday."

"Kidnapped? That's a bit strong a word, don't you think?"

"Well, what would you prefer to call it?" Chris wondered, hoping to extract information. Apparently, Nick knew something too.

"She's being deprogrammed. They'll just talk to her a bit and it'll all be over in a few days. If she wants to go back to you people then, she can. It'll be up to her."

Chris's jaw dropped several inches and his eyes widened. *Being deprogrammed...*his worst fear was now confirmed, thanks to Uncle Nick, who'd been surprisingly helpful.

15 - THE ART OF WAR

We deal with and we defend the rights,
liberty and property of our fellow citizens.
—Johnston, Prichard & Fee, Lawyers. Established 1887

Friday, August 5, 1983

Over a communal breakfast, the occupants of the Parnell house heard the disturbing news of Maree's disappearance as Sarah, Pam and Chris shared their various reports. Reactions ranged from shock and surprise to anger and a sense of being violated and even terrorized. How could someone just take one of their members like that? Was anyone safe?

Since Sarah, who managed the day-to-day running of the center, was anxious to focus her energy on finding Maree, normal activities such as fund-raising and witnessing were put on hold. Members could stay busy doing household chores or spending extra time in the prayer room. Some of the women found books or articles of clothing that belonged to Maree and kept them close by, so they could feel more connected to her. Sarah prayed intensely, for the members, for Maree, for her family, for guidance, insight and help.

Chris had studied Sun Tzu's *The Art of War* and was both an intellectual and a pragmatist. He needed to think and act. He believed in God but also in strategy. His determination to find Maree was strengthened further by knowing that this was a deprogramming attempt, very likely with Americans involved.

Foreigners, coming into our country and picking off our members! How dare they? Bloody Yanks!

He needed to sleep, but his mind was spinning. There were so many different angles that could be explored, Chris realized as he sat back down in the office with a second round of toast and Vegemite.

Second breakfast! I must be a hobbit.

Picking up a pencil, he began to write in a small notepad.

Get back to police.

Consult psychic.

Private investigator.

Talk to Legal folks, NYC.

Talk to Knappy.

Martin Knapp, affectionately known as "Knappy" by some of the church members, was an Auckland lawyer whom the church consulted whenever legal advice was needed.

Concerning the police, Chris decided to call in the missing person report by phone and then follow up in person the next day. After taking care of that, he put a call through to the Legal Affairs department of the Unification Church in New York City.

"Good morning, Kaye! I regret to inform you that another deprogramming is taking place in New Zealand." He filled in the few details that he knew.

"Thanks for calling, Chris. We're naturally concerned for the well-being of your member, but also grateful for being informed," said Kaye from New York. "If this turns out to be the Alexanders, it would be extremely helpful to press charges against them, since they're already on probation."

Chris promised to do his best.

Since it would be good to get an okay from Sarah to pursue his more creative ideas such as consulting with psychics and private eyes, Chris jumped to the last item on the list: *Knappy.*

Martin Knapp had worked for the law firm of Johnston, Prichard and Fee since December 1969 and had been a partner since 1972. Their offices were located in the heart of the central business district of Auckland. He was at his desk when Chris's call came through.

"We have a serious situation," Chris got straight to the point. "One of our Auckland members has gone missing. Her uncle confirms that she's with deprogrammers. They'll be dumping all their crap on her right now, searching for a weak point so they can break her down."

Knapp, immaculate in a three-piece pinstripe business suit, set aside the stack of papers on his desk and sat up straight.

"Good heavens, Chris! This is dreadful! Tell me everything. How did it happen?"

"We think she was taken by her mother and some old friends, using a dinner appointment as bait."

"That would fit the *modus operandi* of American deprogrammers, which you've described to me in the past. The forceful 'snatching' of a victim, with the help of friends or family, followed by confinement."

"Yes, they typically confine victims out of reach of their religious brethren, as well as law enforcement."

"And, during the actual 'snatching,' they're careful to involve friends and/or family members so the perpetrators themselves can evade charges of kidnapping."

Chris grinned. Knapp was great. He remembered everything!

"Yes, exactly! Then, once they're safely away from any possible interference, the perps will relentlessly pummel the victim with ridicule, disinformation, emotional manipulation and so on."

Knapp completed the thought. "With the end goal being to destroy the person's religious faith."

"Precisely, but it gets worse. In some cases, physical violence is part of the treatment. Women victims have been raped. We can only hope that is not happening, but there are no guarantees. I'm really sweating over this. We're racing against time."

"How can I help?"

"Well...let's see, you could start with the police. According to our sisters who paid them a visit, they were less than cooperative; hostile attitude and so on. They're calling it a family matter. But it's obviously a kidnapping where a person's been taken against her will. Perhaps you could approach them from a purely legal angle and see if you can't get a better result?"

Knapp nodded.

"Absolutely. What we're looking at here is Section 209 of the Crimes Act, 1961. That's the law against abduction, which is most likely being violated. The police have a responsibility to act. I'll do whatever I can."

"I know you will." Chris smiled confidently.

"I'll need names, dates, times and any other details you can provide."

Chris reported as thoroughly as he could, while Knapp took notes.

"And Chris, when you go in person to the police, make it clear this is not merely a Missing Persons case. Formally lodge a complaint under Section 209 of the Crimes Act."

"Will do."

After they both hung up, Martin Knapp shook his head and reflected over his past dealings with the Unification Church. He'd always been impressed by these people. They were clean-cut and personable, responsible with their finances and appeared to be of the highest moral character. Yet the public's perception of the group tended to be negative in the extreme.

For example, one year he had been instructed to defend two church members in the Blenheim District Court after they had been charged with "begging". The two were acquitted but the public interest in their case had been very high and not sympathetic.

Later, when the church first filed an application for their premises on St Stephens Avenue in Parnell with the Auckland City Council under the Town and Country Planning Act, there were around 150 notices of opposition to the application. Numerous articles appeared in newspapers and magazines, most of them hostile toward the church, which they usually called a "cult" populated by "Moonies", a pejorative term coined from the name of the church's founder. Knapp rested his chin on one hand and let out a sigh.

It's truly unfortunate that there's always so much prejudice against the church. I certainly hope I can help them in their current dilemma.

Accordingly, he began drafting a carefully worded letter intended for the Auckland police, specifically Assistant Police Commissioner Gibson, whom he knew.

Back at the office in Parnell, Chris thought of one more thing to add to his list:

Talk to newspapers.

16 - FACING NORTH, NEAR THE SEA

When you pass through the waters, I will be with you. And through the rivers, they shall not overwhelm you; when you walk through fire you shall not be burned.
—Isaiah 43:2

Saturday August 6, 1983

Geoff was the first to open the Herald on Saturday morning at the Parnell center. A bold headline announced:

MOONIES SECT SAYS MEMBER MISSING.

Unfortunately, the paper had chosen to use the pejorative term "Moonies" even though Geoff had introduced himself as a spokesperson for the Unification Church. However, it did accurately report the facts as he had presented them.

...Maree Ryan, aged 26, of Parnell, might have been kidnapped on Thursday. The church was told that 'deprogrammers' had taken her, said the spokesman.

"Look at this!" exclaimed Geoff to Chris, Pam and several others at the breakfast table in the upstairs dining room. "Uncle Nick says she's with her mother and brother."

"Mother *and brother!* The plot thickens," remarked Chris. "That Nick has been a mine of information."

"Yes," agreed Geoff, "but he insists that kidnapping is totally the wrong word, *because no harm has come to her.*"

"A likely story," muttered Chris.

Chris and Geoff were old friends who had joined the Church while traveling in England. The two of them had come back to their native New Zealand to see how they might be of assistance to the movement closer to home. With their blond hair and blue eyes, they could have passed for brothers.

On Friday Chris delegated media outreach to Geoff, which proved to be a good move. Chris, with all his righteous passion, could be abrasive and confrontational, where Geoff was gentler and more diplomatic. His boyish good looks were an additional advantage when being interviewed in person.

Consequently, Geoff had spoken to the major daily newspapers that served the Auckland region at that time, *The New Zealand Herald* and the *Auckland Star.*

A little later in the morning, a psychic medium visited the church according to an arrangement set up the previous day by Chris and Sarah.

The woman sat in one of the comfortably furnished downstairs rooms designated for entertaining guests. She looked at a photo of Maree, held a book that belonged to her and an item of clothing, then closed her eyes and concentrated.

After a few moments, the woman said, "She's near the sea...in an isolated place...facing north. There's a house, it's a bach near the sea. Near water... That's all I'm able to tell you. Sorry."

The members thanked her and showed her out.

Sarah was impressed by the woman. "She seems genuine." Chris had mixed feelings.

"Yes, but about 30 percent of all homes in Auckland could be near the ocean facing north, so we would still be looking for a straw in a haystack, given that the population of the city is around a million. And that's assuming the place she's seeing is actually in Auckland rather than elsewhere."

***

Around noon Chris went to the police station to follow up on his Missing Person's report.

"I'd like to lodge a complaint under Section 209 of the Crimes Act."

Once again, Detective Hugglestone was the officer in charge.

"If the woman is with her mother and brother, then she's not going to come to any harm, is she?"

"They're trying to deprogram her, and time is of the essence," argued Chris, eager for the police officer to understand the urgency. "It's an underhanded and draconian method of forced religious conversion. Or de-conversion, as the case may be."

The officer spoke slowly, as though explaining something to a small child. "They're trying to *win her back.* When she eventually surfaces, we will ask her if she has any complaint. In the meantime, this is not a criminal matter, it's a family matter and as such, will be given *low priority.*" He drew out the words for emphasis. "And I for one would appreciate if you would kindly stop wasting our time."

Chris left the police station, shaking his head.

Auckland's finest, indeed. More like bigots with badges!

***

Chris's mentor and ally, Mike Ferris from Scientology, came over early Saturday afternoon. Mike had a good grasp of the situation after his chat with Chris the previous day; he had also read the *Herald* article. Chris filled him in on the latest dealings with the police and the psychic.

"So... no help will be forthcoming from the police, which is not altogether surprising," said Mike. And we know she's with two family members near the sea, facing north. I realize how overwhelming that seems. You might be surprised how much we can narrow down the possibilities by applying a good strategy. How about we start with a map of Auckland?"

They spread out a large map on a desk and huddled around it, looking for all the places that might fit the psychic lady's vision, and drawing small circles around them with a red felt-tip pen. There were many, just as Chris thought: Titirangi, Manukau Harbor, Takapuna, Browns Bay, Whangaparaoa and others.

Pam stepped into the office while Chris and Mike were brainstorming a list of possible people who might be involved in a deprogramming.

Pam sat down with them.

"Former members are usually involved," Mike reminded them, "especially those who have undergone deprogramming."

"Right!" said Chris, his eyes widening. "The vampire syndrome. After you've been bitten, you bite others to stay alive. So, number one would be Bridget Gardner, then how about the one from Christchurch? Menzies, wasn't it?"

"Rosalind Menzies," said Pam.

They made a long list of possible suspects and Pam began looking up a phone number for each name.

Pam's small office, where she usually took care of bookkeeping and secretarial tasks, was rapidly transforming into something resembling a War Room, with maps and lists covering every available surface.

Mike issued further instructions.

"So, Pam, you'll need to call everyone on the list and question them, testing every possibility in order to narrow down the location and the people who might be involved."

"Got it."

***

That evening the *Auckland Star* ran the story on its front page under the headline:

We're doing same as Moonies, says father.

The *Star* had interviewed Maree's father, who offered his personal perspective of what was going on:

This is the first time she's been away from the Moonies for 6½ years. She's quite happy. I haven't spoken to her myself, but I get a ring from her mother each day. I can't tell you where she is, or the Moonies would take her straight back to their outfit.

The Moonies first got hold of her in Adelaide when she went there on a working holiday...she had a great time. We had a letter from her telling us how she was looking forward to coming back. The next letter said she wasn't coming. They must have changed her within a week. They brainwashed her.

You haven't got a show unless you get her on her own. The only way is to play it cool. Get her away. I think a mother has a right to do that. They did the kidnapping in the first place.

We're trying to save one kid. Well, she's an adult now but she went in at 19 and hasn't improved. She's still really a child.

At the bottom of the right-hand corner of the article was a photograph of Maree with her American husband. The caption called him "her church husband".

The final paragraph read:

Auckland police have been investigating but the Star could obtain no comment today.

"Bollocks," said Chris to the members gathered at dinner in the dining room. "The Auckland police haven't done a darn thing."

"That's why they can't comment on their investigation," added Geoff, "because there isn't one."

"What does her father mean, she hasn't improved since she was 19 and she's still a child?" wondered Pam. "Based on what?"

The mood in the room was one of mild amusement mixed with indignation.

"What he's saying is that we're the ones who really do the kidnapping and the brainwashing and somehow we hinder people's development," said Sarah grimly, in response to Pam. "I would say it's quite the opposite in most cases. We grow and change and mature through the *Principle*. But this is just the same stuff they've been tossing at us for years."

Chris flushed, his blue eyes twinkling.

"Same shit, different arsehole."

17 - FREE MAREE

(This case) has been given the lowest of priorities, as far as the police are concerned.
—Detective Inspector G.F. Hugglestone, Auckland Police, to *The New Zealand Herald.*

Monday August 8, 1983

Pam got up early Monday morning when the Parnell house was dark and quiet. Everyone else was sleeping. It was a perfect time to take care of bookkeeping and secretarial tasks without interruption.

At 8 am the phone rang. It was John from the church's legal office in New York City.

"Good morning, Pam. How are you guys doing out there in New Zealand?" He had a kind voice and some of his vowels sounded Canadian.

"Well, the police have been no help. They've been absolutely terrible, so it's up to us to do our own detective work."

"Wow. Unfortunately, it's often the case, that law enforcement and even the justice system tend to look the other way in this type of situation. You probably know that saying, 'Evil flourishes when good men do nothing.' "

"Yes, I do. And we're certainly not doing nothing!"

"Of course not, and we're very grateful to you. Please let us know if there are any developments."

Pam hung up and rubbed her eyes.

"Coffee?" asked Chris, who had just appeared in the doorway.

"Yes, please! You must have read my mind."

Chris disappeared, and Pam took a deep breath.

Time to work on that list some more...

Since Saturday, she'd tried to use every spare minute to work her way meticulously through the long list of possible suspects which she, Chris and his Scientologist friend had created. Over the weekend she'd contacted the Harker family in Napier and spoke to Tim, an ex-member who'd joined in America.

"Do you happen to know anything about Maree Ryan's disappearance?"

"No, actually, I don't. Sorry."

Pam made a note next to Tim's name. *At home in Napier.*

She'd also talked with the mother of Rosalind Menzies, who lived in Christchurch. The woman sounded elderly and frail.

"Rosalind is not here, she's on holiday. I urged her to get some rest and relaxation, for her health. She has a thyroid condition, you know."

"No, I didn't know."

"And you church people really shouldn't be calling and bothering her."

Pam wrote: *Ros Menzies "on holiday."*

It was time to call the Gardners. Bridget Gardner was an interesting character who had gone through a deprogramming. She considered herself an ex-member, yet maintained a friendly relationship with the church, as if she were in two minds. Pam pondered that as she dialed the number and waited.

Torn between heart and head, perhaps? We know Maree's not at your lake house in Taupo, but are you involved in some other way?

"Hello?" It was Bridget.

"Hi, Bridget, it's Pam from the church. I'm calling about Maree Ryan's disappearance and probable kidnapping. Would you happen to know anything about that?"

Silence.

"Bridget, are you there?"

"Yes, I'm here."

"So, what do you know about it?"

"Well, if I knew anything, I wouldn't be able to talk about it." Her voice was strained.

"Are you involved in some way?" Pam probed.

"Maybe, but like I said, I can't really talk about it." Bridget giggled nervously, followed by more silence.

"I see." Pam hung up the phone, eyes wide with curiosity. Suddenly she wasn't sleepy any more.

Next to Bridget's name, she drew several large asterisks and wrote: *Evasive, suspicious!*

Chris reappeared with a mug in each hand and took a seat across from Pam on the other side of her desk. He passed her a mug of hot coffee.

"How's it going?"

"Very interesting! I just talked to Bridget Gardner. I think she knows something."

"Really?" Chris smiled and nodded thoughtfully. "We'll need to keep an eye on that young lady." He picked up a copy of the Yellow Pages and set it in front of him.

"What are you looking for?"

"Just between you, me and a couple of others, Private Investigators in Auckland." Pam chuckled at Chris's conspiratorial tone.

Pam had just taken a sip of coffee when the phone rang. She picked up.

"It's a TV reporter for you." Chris took the receiver.

"Is Maree still missing?" asked the reporter.

"Yes. We have no idea where she is, and we're extremely concerned."

"What do you think is going on?"

"We believe she's been taken by criminals who wish to destroy her faith through coercion and manipulation."

"We understand that the Auckland Police have dropped the case to lowest priority, and they've accused you of wasting police time. Would you care to comment on that?"

"Of course! A woman has been taken somewhere against her will. This is highly illegal, yet the police are choosing to turn a blind eye, instead of upholding the law."

"So, you're now seeking legal advice?"

"We are talking to a solicitor to find out what our legal options are."

***

At the offices of Johnston, Prichard and Fee in downtown Auckland, Martin Knapp was looking over a letter intended for the office of Bryan Gibson, Assistant Police Commissioner:

I have reason to believe the disappearance of Maree Ryan is more than simply a family affair, as the Auckland police have been publicly insisting. I believe an American 'deprogramming' team is involved which includes a Joseph Alexander Junior, who has a conviction for kidnapping in Colorado; the other American, Joseph Alexander Senior, is wanted by the U.S. District Attorney's office in another state on a charge of suspected kidnapping. To emphasize this concern, I have in my possession a copy of the aforementioned conviction notice.

May I also bring to your attention Section 209 of the law against kidnapping, which stipulates that

"Everyone is liable to imprisonment for a term not exceeding 14 years who unlawfully carries off or detains any person without his consent, or with his consent obtained by fraud or duress, with intent...to cause him to be confined or imprisoned."

The person or persons who have taken and are holding Maree, presumably against her will, are guilty of violating the law, regardless of whether they are her family members.

I urge the police to act in accordance with the law and without allowing themselves to be affected by personal animosity toward the parties involved or by biased views promoted in the popular press.

Finally, this case raises the question of the individual's right to religious freedom, which is a fundamental principle of our democratic society. Law enforcement authorities have a responsibility to protect such fundamental rights, and therefore to apply the law universally, without bias.

Yours faithfully,

Martin Knapp,

Johnston, Prichard and Fee, solicitors.

He handed the letter to a secretary, still reflecting on its contents.

When the police become selective about where they apply the law, it's the thin edge of the wedge.

***

Meanwhile, at church headquarters, Peter and Mark were in the back yard. They were practical, hands-on fellows who, when they weren't in Parnell doing church activities, worked on a coastal cray-fishing business in the Wairarapa region.

Peter was frustrated.

"Since we're not directly involved in the search for our sister, I feel like I should be doing something."

"Yeah, we can't just do nothing," Mark agreed.

"What if we had a big public protest, with signs and lots of noise, downtown near the Mayor's office or hey, what about outside the police station?" Peter's blue eyes lit up at the thought.

"Yeah, that'd be awesome. Let's at least make some signs and we can figure out the other details later."

"Okay, I know where there's some paint and some poster-board."

The pair got to work, authoring slogans and painting them on placards.

Deprogramming is faith-breaking!

Deprogrammers are criminals!

Religious freedom for all!

One of the signs said simply, *Free Maree!*

***

On their way to meet with the Private Investigator, Chris tried to explain to Pam the reasons for the strict confidentiality.

"Did you see the headline in tonight's *Star*? *Moonies See Lawyers*, as though that's something sinister. Next thing you know, it'll be *Moonies See Private Eye*, if we don't keep this under wraps. We're perfectly within our rights to see a solicitor or a private detective, but anything *we* do gets twisted the wrong way or blown out of proportion. You know how that goes."

Pam sighed. She knew very well how it went.

"In the minds of the public, the media and even some of the members, Private Investigators are part of a sleazy underworld where good people fear to tread. We're just steering clear of any possible backlash."

Pam nodded.

They stopped at the edge of Victoria Park near the old gasworks building, a part of town that was usually quiet and deserted, then walked toward the designated meeting point. The sun was beginning to set, casting long shadows across the cut grass.

Pam felt excited. "This feels very clandestine!"

"That's the general idea."

They'd only waited a few seconds when Tai appeared. He was tall, clean-shaven, brown-skinned and carried himself with athletic grace and the dignified bearing of a military man. Pam recalled Chris saying he was Mormon and had been in the special forces.

Chris had explained the general situation to Tai over the phone. Now he shared photographs of Maree, documents about prominent deprogrammers, names and locations of potential suspects.

"One of our suspects has just risen to the top of the list!" Chris handed Tai a sheet of Bridget's known details.

Tai looked at it and nodded slowly. He shook both of their hands firmly, making eye contact. "I'll do whatever I can. You can expect daily updates from me." Then he disappeared into the shadows.

"Not at all what I expected!" Pam commented on the drive back to Parnell.

"Rather impressive," said Chris. "Probably plays a mean game of rugby!"

IMAGES

My Cell

28·12·75
DAD

The Coal Range

The Ryan kids, circa 1968
Back row: Anne, Pat, Paul
Front: Maree, Josephine, Genevieve, Christine

My first flat - Clarendon St. - Dunedin

Sundial Umbrella
Invercargill

Korean culture night - Sydney

Maree Ryan with her church husband, Mr. Bob Gauper after their wedding at a mass ceremony in the United States (Auckland Star, August, 1983 (Reconstructed)

Maree Ryan with her church husband, Mr Bob Gauper, after their wedding at a mass ceremony in the United States.

New Yorker Hotel
1982

Monday, August 15, 1983

Auckland Star

HOME EDITION

Captive cultist blocks her ears to deprogramming

Moonie: 'I felt like an animal in a cage'

'saved' ...ies

MOONIE CLAIM LOW ON LIST

Withdrawal of Moonie going well says family

No Action Against Family

Maree Ryan, ... member of the ... the

Moonies see lawyers

Moonie leader Mr Chris Newman says he will take legal advice to step up efforts to locate "kidnapped" Unification C... membe... Ry...

handed over to her mother.

She was ...

...ve believe she ...rogrammed.

...lack of help ...g mean that ...port deprog-

Missing Moonie

August 1983, Headlines

"Church husband" meets the in-laws

Sister's wedding - 1984

18 - THE RING

But nothing was the same ever again—not after that day when I cried. I cried it all out that day, emptied myself of everything but a stupendous rage...I carried that rage in me like an iron heart.
—Victor Herman, *Coming out of the Ice.*

Monday, August 8

I lay on the bed for a long time. No one bothered me, which allowed me time to calm down and reflect. As I lay there the molten anger and frustration, some of which had recently erupted, began to harden into a new inner strength and resolve.

I still didn't know how I would get out of there. I had no idea if anyone was looking for me or even if they were, how they would be able to find me.

But the person who sat up on the bed that day was a different person from the one who had lain down. She was fierce and battle-hardened. She would not let those people beat her. They had no right! She would do whatever it took to beat them.

Why did I even eat their food every day? It was the food of control, like meals served by a warden to a prisoner, or feed given to an animal in a cage.

That's what I am, an animal in a cage. I should be throwing their stupid food back in their faces.

Then I knew what to do. I would stop eating. I had fasted before and could do it again. *"A man doesn't live by bread alone..." said Jesus.*

I had never been very good at fasting. As a Catholic child, even the three hours fast before Communion had been difficult for me as it meant going to 9:30 am Mass without breakfast. Before Mass was over, I was dizzy and anxious.

Fasting in the Unification Church was a serious business. Along with prayer, study and sexual purity, it was a way to deny the body and strengthen the spirit. It was not unusual for members to offer a three- or seven-day fast, the latter being one of the conditions required to prepare for the marriage Blessing.

I did a three-day fast during my early days in the church as a fulltime member of the Melbourne center. After the first twenty-four hours I felt nauseous and threw up green bile. Christa, our German missionary and center leader, gave me mineral water but I couldn't keep it down. I thought for certain she would want me to cancel the fast since I felt so miserable. To my dismay, she kindly but firmly encouraged me to finish what I'd started, and I did survive through the next two days.

I knew that fasting would not kill me and would help me. I just had to decide how long. I could limit it to twenty-four hours and avoid the nausea, but that seemed too easy. Besides, what would it matter if I got sick? It wasn't as if I was doing anything productive. A little green bile might be exciting...like a scene from *The Exorcist...* yet three days seemed daunting. I was feeling determined, but not sure if I had the strength of will for three days of fasting. So, I considered forty hours.

If Jesus could fast forty days, I can fast forty hours.

It would make me stronger spiritually and, if I lost a few pounds, I would look better for the TV cameras when I finally could get out of this place!

I did the math. I'd stopped eating by 9 am because that was when Joe had come in and started his raving. 9 am tomorrow would be twenty-four hours, 9 pm would be thirty-six; four more would take me to 1 am the following morning. I could do that. I *would* do that, I determined and silently offered it up.

Someone brought lunch.

"No, thank you, take it away." I went back to lying down on the bed. I would accept nothing but water.

Later someone brought dinner. It was meat loaf and mashed potatoes on a paper plate and it smelled delicious. Hunger pangs had started gnawing at my insides, and the food was tempting, but my mind was made up.

"No thank you, take it away."

Thankfully, they did take it away, which removed the temptation.

I heard my mother's voice in the hallway. "You need to eat *some*thing."

"No, I don't." I wasn't fasting to torment my mother, but if it made her uncomfortable, that was her problem, not mine.

A little later, Rosalind came in with a plastic tumbler of water.

"Are you not feeling well?" Rosalind had been a medical student at the same university I went to. I could imagine her as a doctor; she had a gentle bedside manner.

"I'm fine. I just don't want to eat anything."

"Okay. Make sure you drink plenty of water. Your Mum is really worried about you."

I scoffed. "She thinks I'm fat anyway. Tell her I'll be losing a few kilos." Rosalind smiled kindly and left.

As the plump daughter of a thin woman, I had struggled tremendously throughout my teen years with feelings of shame and inferiority. For Mum, weight loss was so simple: if she gained a few pounds after a pregnancy, she took no sugar in her tea for a few weeks and *voila!* the weight came off. She would tell us, with a shrug, "You just have to burn more calories than you take in!"

As a teen, I sometimes ate to block out the painful emotions associated with being overweight, or the bitter frustrations and despair over diet or exercise regimens that never seemed to work. I knew on some subconscious level that weight problems were complex: they were emotional, spiritual. There were different body types and differing metabolic rates. But for my accountant mother, it was a simple matter of mathematics.

***

That night I had a dream. It was about a ring. In real life, I wore three rings: my gold Blessing ring with the twelve-gate symbol on my right ring finger; and on my left hand, a plain sterling silver ring as well as a silver cubic zirconia. The last had been a gift from my husband, Bob, who was still in America waiting to join me after our betrothal period was over. We were managing our long-distance relationship by exchanging letters and an occasional phone call; and sometimes by the exchanging of gifts. Bob had sent me some lovely things, including the gold-plated watch I was wearing and recently the sparkly silver ring, which I cherished.

In the dream, the silver cubic zirconia was not on my finger but suspended in mid-air. It gave off a bright light like an aura. As I watched in awe, it became larger and brighter until it seemed like the ring and its brilliant light were filling up an entire room.

It was one of those dreams that you never forget. The next morning, I remembered not just the image of the ring, but the feeling that accompanied it — a warm, bright, hopefulness, and thoughts of Bob, since clearly, the dream was about him. It was telling me, "Remember Bob! Remember the person who gave you the ring!" It made me smile.

Of course, I remembered him. I missed him. I wished he could come and be my hero and save me from this crazy situation. I wondered if he even knew I was missing. In any case, I knew through his words and gifts that he was committed to our Blessing, as was I

Mary, Bridget, Rosalind and the others might abandon their Blessings and divorce their spouses. Not I, no matter how much they tried to confuse or intimidate me. To me, being faithful to commitments was an essential part of good character. I would finish what I'd started.

19 - BOB

People should marry across national and cultural boundaries with people from countries they consider to be their enemies so that the world of peace can come that much more quickly.
—Sun Myung Moon

June 24, 1982

I first met Bob in the Grand Ballroom of the New Yorker Hotel in New York City which at the time, was also the World Mission Center of the Unification Church. We were introduced to each other by the Reverend Moon himself.

People always ask me if there were extensive interviews or personality profiles like you might find on *eharmony* or *match.com.* No, not really. Rev. Moon was extraordinary and spiritually gifted. Some said he could look at a person's face and understand what kind of ancestors you had, what kind of character you had and what kind of spouse might complement you. He matched opposites together to balance them out, trying to pair combinations that would produce well-rounded children.

Early in my church life Tanya had told me that Rev. Moon would pick out a husband for us if we wanted him to, once we'd been members for three and a half years and were at least 22 years of age. I thought it sounded like a wonderful idea. I had seen enough of flirting, dating and the silly games people played.

Some of the older sisters had already been matched back in 1980 and I was so envious. Susan had a lovely fiancé, Ashleigh from England. I could tell she was crazy about him. Tanya was engaged to a Japanese missionary in Mexico. It was so exciting to think it was finally my turn.

About 25 of us had flown over from Australia to New York together because there was going to be a Marriage Blessing ceremony as well as a matching. Around half of our group were those who had been previously matched and engaged and would join their fiancés for the group wedding planned for July 1, while the rest were single members like me who were hoping to be matched and join the Blessing ceremony. Late June was hot and muggy in Manhattan, but we didn't care! It was my first time in America, ever. Everything was new, different and exhilarating.

My friend Josephine and I shared Room 3306 with other Australian sisters at the New Yorker Hotel. The rooms were undergoing a remodeling process and there were construction materials lying here and there. Parts of the wall were missing and we'd brought sleeping bags, knowing there would be no beds. We didn't care! We were going to be matched by Reverend Moon!

On the afternoon the matching was to take place, Josephine asked me what I was going to wear.

"Um...Tanya gave me these two dresses. Maybe the pink one?" It was a flattering, belted dress made of a good-quality opaque fabric except for the shoulders and sleeves which were chiffon. It seemed a little fancier than the silky green. I chose the pink and felt good in it, encouraged by the special "minimizer" bra I'd found at Macy's and the double-layer control top pantyhose which helped me not to feel fat.

Earlier that day, we sat on the carpeted floor of the Grand Ballroom along with hundreds of other members from five continents. It was a gorgeous place that had been recently remodeled with phoenix birds ornately molded in white plaster, surrounding raised images of the twelve-gate symbol. Reverend Moon spoke for several hours to help us prepare our minds and hearts for the matching process. Smiling as he spoke about the importance of marriage, family and living for the sake of others, he urged us not to be superficial.

Looking at the brothers he joked (through a translator), "What if I give you a large sister with rich bosom and hip?" I blushed at the words bosom and hip, hoping no one would notice.

"You can use her as a pillow!" Everyone laughed.

And to us women he said, "The blessing of marriage is what's important, not how handsome the man is. Even if he's as ugly as an Idaho potato!" We laughed more.

"A man should be unchanging and faithful. It doesn't matter if he's ugly! You should be grateful even if I match you to Elephant Man."

Josephine and I giggled nervously as we received the fatherly advice. I'd always fallen for good-looking men, but who knows what kind of character they had?

Later I would describe the day's events in my diary:

Father came to the Grand Ballroom about 10:30 am and spoke to us for about 3 hours. He talked about the lightning of true love and how it's good to match people who are like polar opposites. A tall man should marry a short woman, and so on. 'If a long nose man marries a long nose woman, they'll have children like Pinocchio!'

We took a break for lunch about 1:30 and were told to come back at 3 pm. Josephine and I stuck together most of the time. I bumped into Carl (English missionary to Australia) and we had lunch. He took one look at my pink dress and said, 'You can't wear that! Father will freak out if he sees you in that, it's see-through!'

After eating I raced upstairs to put on the green silky one with the puff sleeves and fitted waist. One of the ribbons was out and I nearly panicked because it was getting close to 3 pm. Had to calm down so I could fix the dress and get ready. I was about 15 minutes late but at least I avoided an emotional meltdown.

Father hadn't arrived yet, but he did soon. It's amazing when Father comes into the Grand Ballroom. It seems that the whole room fills up with white light. Was someone adjusting the lighting or was it some spiritual phenomenon? I don't know.

I was in the back of the Ballroom but could hear people laughing, shouting and cheering as Father walked down the middle of the Ballroom, nudging and pushing members to either side to make an aisle between the brothers and the sisters. It was like Moses parting the Red Sea.

He was wearing a casual open-neck shirt and mostly had his hands in his pockets, but his look was one of intense concentration. I saw a mischievous half-smile on his face and a kind of twinkle in his eye. I can still see it now.

He started by asking, 'Who wants international matching?'

I raised my hand. A Korean was what I was hoping for, having been in love with Korea since my early days in the church when I first tasted kimchi and listened to Arirang...

Then he asked for male and female representatives from many different nations: Korea, Japan, America, Germany, France, Italy, Switzerland, Austria, Australia, New Zealand... I stood up when he asked for New Zealand sisters. He walked up and down the aisle, then pointed to me and said something like, 'You go up.' I pointed to myself, glanced behind me and asked the question, 'Me?' Since no one behind me was standing, he must have meant me, so I moved forward nervously and stood in the line of sisters who were facing a line of brothers on the opposite side of the aisle.

I recognized some of the brothers, vaguely wondering why there were two Australians standing (shouldn't there be only one?) as I mentally prepared myself to be matched to anyone in that line. But it soon became apparent that Father wasn't just pairing people from the two lines to each other. In some cases, he would look out to those still sitting down and match one of them to a person in the line.

And that's what happened to me. Father went and picked a round-faced, stocky, red-haired brother from among those seated and called me out to join him in the middle of the aisle. We had to bow in front of Mother Moon and Ye-Jin, the eldest daughter. Mother was smiling at us and looking extremely beautiful and radiant.

We went upstairs to the balcony area to 'discuss'. The red-head asked, 'Do you love God and True Parents?' and as soon as I said 'Yes' he got up to leave as if that was all he needed to know. Was he even going to ask if I accepted the match or not? Apparently not, so I quickly said, 'It's OK with me,' and we went back downstairs, signed our names in the registration book, got our cards stapled together, bowed to Father, who was still matching, then to Mother again, right down to the ground, then made our way out of the Ballroom. On the way out, I was briefly interviewed by Tony Colombrito of the News World newspaper.

We were unexpectedly greeted in the lobby by a crowd of cheering brothers and sisters with flashing cameras. We were hugged and congratulated and photographed many times. The red-head's name was Bob. He was American and captain of a Mobile Fundraising team (MFT). Bob bought me a carnation and introduced me to Mike, his spiritual father, who was selling the carnations and had a Home Church area in the Bronx.

At first Bob didn't know what to say. He was a bit shy. He did say that he didn't talk at all before he joined the church. I can't say that I instantly fell in love with him, but I'm glad because I feel from past experiences that those emotions can be untrustworthy. I would rather our relationship grows gradually and naturally. The main thing is that this is the person whom

Father gave to me. How can I not accept him? I trusted the wisdom of Father's choice.

We watched a few more couples come out. They must have been local New York members as they were cheered even more riotously than we had been.

After a while we went down Eighth Avenue for coffee and talked a bit. Bob joined the church in Seattle but he's from Marysville, California. He can cook well, trained to be a chef and cooks most of the meals for his fundraising team.

We came back and had dinner in the New Yorker. We later learned that Father was matching until 9 pm, took a break until 10:30, then kept matching until 3 am. As we ate, we could hear intermittent loud cheers from the lobby as the new couples emerged. Most Australians and Kiwis didn't get matched until toward the end, so I felt privileged to have been among the first. We were the fourth couple to register, out of hundreds. About midnight I went up to my room, so exhausted that I fell asleep in my green dress and didn't wake until 5 am.

20 - A WHIRLWIND COURTSHIP

Radio interviewer: *"Wasn't it hard for you to marry a virtual stranger?"*
Me: *"Well, these days a girl might meet a man in a bar and be sleeping with him that same night. All we did was get married."*

Bob and I were engaged for exactly one week before the big wedding.

We tend to do things differently in the Unification Church. In our case we were engaged, then we courted and got married, courted some more and finally moved in together much later and consummated the marriage. Our way had more in common with ancient Jewish betrothal practices than modern Western marriage.

Maree's diary, Friday June 25th, 1982

Father was matching today until about 4 in the afternoon. Those already matched had to "stand by" for an announcement about the Holy Wine Ceremony. I found out that Josephine was matched to a black brother from Sudan and she's very pleased! Trevor, James and nearly all the Australian brothers got matched to Japanese sisters, most of whom don't speak any English.

The Holy Wine Ceremony was something like a mix of Communion and Baptism, a mystical sacramental event, representing the cleansing of Original Sin for our lineage. It also signified our official engagement.

The brief ceremony took place in the hot and crowded Grand Ballroom. At least one sister fainted. Bob and I faced each other with our hands placed one over the other, symbolizing True Parents' hands embracing our own. Father prayed while elders brought trays with thimble-size containers of Holy Wine and we drank it. Bob was so nervous he almost forgot to pass the cup back to me.

Afterward, we went to the 4th floor to get our photos taken along with other members from the Chicago region. Someone said, "He's a really good brother!" We had dinner downstairs with a group of couples from my region, Oceania (Australia, New Zealand, and the South Pacific islands). Bob seems more at ease in a group such as this rather than one-on-one. I must admit that I do, too.

Saturday June 26

Bob took me to a diner on Eighth Avenue for breakfast. I ordered bacon and eggs.

"Scrambledsunnysideuporover?"

"What?"

"Scrambledsunnysideuporover?" This time the waitress sounded annoyed and luckily Bob rescued me.

"She just wants to know how you'd like your eggs. Scrambled, fried, or fried and turned over."

That was my first cultural experience of the day. Later I would experience my first black church.

I had attended a Mobilization meeting in the Bamboo Room earlier in the day, where a state leader encouraged everyone to participate in some public outreach. I accepted an interfaith assignment to visit churches in the Bronx and invite local ministers to our wedding and was glad when Bob agreed to help.

To get to the Bronx, we caught the subway train from Penn Station which is directly beneath Madison Square Garden. The unexpected smells of vomit and stale urine on the subway staircases and platforms turned my stomach sour and I briefly worried that I might lose my New York breakfast. The train itself was almost completely full of black people. I was surprised. I'd never seen so many black people in my life.

We got off at the Bronx. I saw huge apartment buildings, kids playing in the streets, people walking by with large portable stereo sets, the kind that are called "ghetto blasters." I guessed we must be in the ghetto. Everyone we saw was either black or brown. "Probably Jamaican or Puerto Rican," said Bob.

I was glad to get to spend time with Bob, so I could know him better and feel more connected. Now that I'd seen the Bronx up close, I was really glad to be with him. A former wrestler, he was a well-built young man with strong shoulders and powerful looking upper body, not unlike some of the rugby players I admired as a teenager.

We found a few churches but nothing much was going on. After all, it was Saturday. After walking around, we heard music, *live* music, coming from outside a small church.

A band was playing on the sidewalk to a small crowd. Women in the crowd were wearing Sunday-best clothes and a singer was belting out some Gospel song. A gray haired, middle aged man with a clerical collar was sitting nearby, singing, clapping, and smiling. We exchanged greetings and introductions.

"Welcome, praise God! I am Pastor Joseph Worrell of the Mount Calvary Church of God in Christ!" He ushered us into the nearby church building.

"Let's go inside where we can *hear* each other, above all this joyful noise!"

As it turned out, Pastor Worrell and his congregation were in the midst of a 24-hour prayer meeting.

A 24-hour prayer meeting? I had never heard of such a thing, in all my life as a Catholic or a Unificationist. I was impressed.

"Yes, it is still going on, praise God. I see so much sin in this world, so much *filth*, and it bothers me, it really bothers me! Because *sin* is *filth!* And I can't do nothing about it except to preach holiness, praise God; and I don't do it for money, praise God. Because, if someone was to give me a million dollars, praise God, and tell me not to preach holiness, I would just say take your million dollars, praise God, and let me go on preachin' the holy word of God, praise God."

Pastor Worrell was inspired to hear about our international, interracial mass wedding and was quite interested in attending. He also said it was okay for us to come back and speak at his Sunday Service the next day. We were delighted.

In the warm afterglow of our memorable experience with Reverend Worrell, Bob and I had a little Bronx picnic on a corner outside a gas station where we found a small triangle of green grass. We shared American cheese with crackers and orange juice before heading back to Manhattan on the subway.

The Australian brothers who were staying at the New Yorker had a much larger room than mine and it was more finished. I'd heard they even had their own coffee. Since Bob had meetings to attend, I decided to go to the Australian brothers' room and ask for some coffee. While there, I had a good chat with James, a tall brother with a prominent nose, who said the Australians he was sitting with during the matching had given a huge cheer when they saw me being matched to Bob!

James told me he was very pleased with his fiancée, Tsuneko, although he was a bit worried.

"I feel like I'm not good enough for her. And I'm afraid she thinks she's not good enough for me, since so many people keep telling her what a good brother I am!"

I had met Tsuneko and she was charming; cute and pretty.

Before I could respond, another Aussie brother, Trevor, came into the room smiling broadly and carrying a "Happy Bell Doll" which his fiancée Kazuko had given him, along with some sweet little photos of herself. Another brother came in with a bigger Japanese doll given to him by his fiancée Michiko. These tough, macho guys were so happy and inspired by their dainty Japanese wives and their dainty Japanese presents. The incongruity was both funny and incredibly moving at the same time. I felt a surge of joy and gratitude, that God, through Father, had given these tough brothers such beautiful women to be their wives. My heart overflowed with love for these guys that I'd worked with and fought with and taken for granted so much in the past. Thirty-six years later, these couples are still together and having raised their families, are now looking forward to their grandchildren.

When I got back to my room, Bob had left a note on my door, to meet him at 9 am tomorrow.

I still have that note.

Diary, Sunday June 27th

I'd overslept and missed the 7am meeting in the Bamboo Room.

"I feel so guilty!" I told Bob when we met.

"Don't worry, it's okay," he assured me.

I've always been highly strung, "a temperamental artist," my mother would say. I tend to get upset easily over many small things. Bob isn't like that. He seems steady and calm, a good sign for us as a couple.

We attended Pastor Worrell's service at 11:30 am in the Bronx. It was a spirit-filled occasion, with singing, dancing, tambourines, testimony, and a lot of praising God. It went on for three hours.

Pastor Worrell gave a fiery sermon about encouragement.

"I know I have to be out savin' souls on the street, not just standin' in my pulpit all day. We oughta work hard, until we're tired, really tired, tired for the Lord, tired because I'm savin' souls, praise God."

I was humbled and moved by this man's dedication.

Bob spoke to the congregation about our wedding and invited everybody. I was impressed by how well he spoke and felt proud to be supporting him.

Then we all sang "Marching to Zion, beautiful, beautiful Zion" from the hymn books. I had never heard the song before. It seemed like one of the loveliest hymns I'd ever heard. I felt sure I would never forget it. Before leaving I hugged and kissed some of the ladies who had shared their testimonies of how they'd been saved as they had really touched my heart.

Back "home" in Manhattan, we went to a Chinese restaurant on 34th St where over lunch, Bob told me more about his family, and I learned that his parents had moved to California from Minnesota, coincidentally where I'd spent a 7-hour layover on my flight to NYC. They were from Norwegian and Swedish ancestry, which (I guess) explains Bob's red hair and broad cheek-bones. So...I was about to marry a Viking! How exciting! Also, I found out that his grandparents did not like Catholics. The same ugly tail-piece of a roast bird which my parents called the parson's nose, Bob's Grandpa called the Pope's nose. In that sense, I was marrying into enemy lineage which we trusted to be a short-cut to world peace. But what on earth would my parents think?

My parents! I needed to write them a long letter and let them know what I was doing. So, after we sat in the New Yorker lobby for a while, I told Bob I needed to go to the Deli-Sun, a church-owned, fast food place next-door to the New Yorker. I could sit at a table there, drink coffee and try to think how to break the news to my family that I was now engaged and about to be married.

I sat down in the Deli-Sun at a comfortable booth and tried to write.

"Dear Mum and Dad, I'm in New York, met a nice man called Bob and I'm going to marry him on Thursday..." just wouldn't be right. It was so hard to explain to them. I prayed to Heavenly Father to help me find the right words and the right heart. I'd barely finished praying when Trina, one of my Australian friends, sat down next to me with a big smile on her face and said, "There's someone here you need to meet." Then she introduced me to a couple around my parents' age who had just arrived from New Zealand. Their names were Rex and Bev and they were in New York to attend the wedding at Madison Square Garden and they had three children

who joined the church. Three! But there was something so different about these people that felt fresh and new and wonderful. They were happy for their children! They even said they'd heard of me and were warm and kind and glad to meet me. They said they'd try and look up my parents sometime when they got back to New Zealand.

I sat back down to write again with fresh power, inspiration, and confidence.

Tuesday June 29th

Shopped for shoes, slips, and gloves. Macy's almost sold out of long white slips! Shoe stores were almost out of white shoes and white sandals. After a lot of walking, I finally found some sandals.

Stood in long lines for veils and blessing rings.

Wednesday June 30th

Wedding Rehearsal at Madison Square Garden

21 - THE WEDDING

> *(Since) arranged marriages have a proven record...tell you what, let's make a bet—Rev Moon's matches against the national average rate of divorce. We'll get back together in the year 2000. If I lose, I'll eat Rev. Moon's front door. If you lose, you have to join the moonies.*
> **—Larry Moffitt, *News World Sunday Magazine, January 1981***

June 30, 1982

On the day of our wedding rehearsal, I met Bob in the downstairs lobby of the New Yorker Hotel and together we walked the short distance to Madison Square garden along Eighth Avenue. We were with Mike, Bob's spiritual father, and his fiancée Monika, a pretty, dark-haired German missionary to the Bahamas. Since we hadn't eaten breakfast, Mike shared his apple and grapefruit with us. Mike was a good-looking, extroverted guy who talked a lot, which was a good thing because Bob and I were still awkward and shy and didn't always know what to talk about.

We practiced our processional along with the other four thousand-plus brides and grooms. While it seemed like a mind-boggling, logistical impossibility to me, to organize that many people, somehow it did work, although it seemed to take forever as we walked side by side, four couples wide, through the stadium entrance from the Felt Forum, over the stage and into the huge auditorium.

"Make sure your lines as well as rows are all neatly aligned!" barked one of the elders in charge of line-straightening. After checking and adjusting our formations, we stood still as the color guard entered, a procession of flag-bearers from our seventy nations. I smiled, realizing that I knew many of the flag-bearers by name since they were friends or fiancés of friends. There was Jim from New Zealand, Mike from Australia, Daniel from Ghana, Taj from Sudan, Jacob from Cameroon, Peki from Western Samoa and others.

Then it was time for the recessional. We exited the auditorium over the stage and back into the Felt Forum, where we were scolded by Col Bo Hi Pak, a Korean elder.

"It must be perfect, like the Columbia Space Shuttle launching! You have to walk into the hall with dignity, not with zero attitude! Now please do it again."

After an exhausting Round Two of processional/color guard/recessional, Col Pak was satisfied.

"Okay, this time you walked with beautiful solemnity, not like before! I am deeply proud of you and so grateful to work with you. Now please collect your box lunch from the Rotunda."

Over lunch I chatted with Bob about folk music and ballads, genres which we both loved. I looked forward to someday sharing with him some of my favorite Australian folk songs. I also learned more about Bob's spiritual father.

"Mike's mom is really negative. He's been kidnapped three times. But he's pretty tough, he was a football jock in high school and he just kept escaping. One time it took three guys to hold him down in the back of a van."

"Wow."

After an afternoon nap at the New Yorker, I met Bob again for dinner on the 29th floor which I guessed was reserved for MFT leaders, some of whom were Japanese. When I got there, Bob was talking to some small Japanese children and I was touched to see how kindly and naturally he related to them. He must have told them, "I'm waiting for my fiancée," because one little girl, who looked to be about three, kept parroting those words.

"I'm waiting for my fiancée! I'm waiting for my fiancée!" she chanted.

The kids had made a mess on the hallway floor. Bob picked up and cleaned up after them with superb efficiency. It occurred to me that he might be doing it just to impress me, but even if that was true, it worked. At that moment I thought, this is probably how he cleans the back of his MFT van. It showed an earnest heart, a humble mind. Heart of the Father, shoes of a servant. And I believed in my own heart that this was the person God had prepared for me, recognizing in him a basic purity and goodness.

After dinner we went our separate ways as I had to do some ironing. Carl had asked me to iron his suit, so I went to Rm 1614, one of the few rooms with an iron and ironing board. There was already a long line, so I stood at the end of the queue waiting patiently for my turn. Some Mexican sisters arrived after me but were so aggressive that I let them in front of me. By 11:30 pm I still hadn't ironed Carl's suit and he came knocking on the door. I opened it, exhausted and almost in tears.

He looked at me with brotherly concern.

"Is everything okay between you and Bob?"

"Yes, it's fine! If only I could get to the ironing board!"

July 1, 1982

We dressed in our rooms. I helped Josephine with her makeup. It was the first time she'd worn makeup in her whole life! I was just putting on my veil when Bob knocked on the door.

We went down the elevator which was stuffed to the seams with brides and grooms. The hotel lobby was a boiling sea of wall-to-wall people. You could barely move. I almost lost Bob when he went to collect my posy of flowers. There were announcements over the P.A. system:

"If you are ready, please go to the Felt Forum. Do NOT stay in the lobby! Repeat, do NOT stay in the lobby!"

The next one made me smile:

"If anyone has misplaced their spouse, please go to the Grand Ballroom!"

Luckily Bob appeared shortly, and I was glad that I didn't need to go looking for him among the Lost and Found Spouses.

On our way down Eighth Avenue a barrier and police guard separated us from the crowds of onlookers who had gathered to see the unlikely spectacle of hundreds of couples in white wedding dresses and navy suits straggling toward Madison Square Garden down a New York City block.

I detected no hostility from the crowd. New Yorkers were rather amused or even inspired by the sight of us.

One man said to a reporter, "You don't see a lot of young people getting married these days. This is nice. This is beautiful."

We had to wait in the Felt Forum quite a while, but luckily there were seats. An elder brother named Dan Fefferman was there to organize us. He also entertained us with a song and a funny story about an American member who once attempted to show off his Korean language skills to Reverend Moon. He couldn't understand why Father and the Korean elders laughed so hard at him, since his pronunciation was quite good. Then someone explained that what he'd actually said was, "Are you ready to eat Mr. Kim?"

Finally, we were instructed to move off into the Rotunda, where each bride had to take a carnation from her bouquet and place it in her groom's lapel. Around the perimeter of the Rotunda there were "grooming stations" supplying mirrors, makeup, Kleenex, ginseng, aspirin and whatever other emergency supplies the elder sisters had been able to think of. A cheerful Korean lady brushed some powder onto my cheeks.

"Need more color!" She had to raise her voice to be heard above the buzz of so many conversations.

Then she helped Monika with her veil.

Suddenly all the chatter stopped, like the flip of a switch, and some people had begun to quietly hum Holy Song Number 36, in unison. A brother whispered to us that Father had arrived in the building and therefore it was almost time for the ceremony to begin.

It was surreal. We were like the crowd scene in a new epic movie as we solemnly moved into the auditorium, side by side, four couples at a time, to the tune of Mendelssohn's Wedding March alternating with Holy Song No. 36, *Song of the Banquet*, played by an unseen orchestra.

The huge arena had been magically transformed overnight. Snowy white carpet covered the entire floor and as we processed over the now red-carpeted platform, True Parents sprinkled us with holy water.

We took our places in the second row of the main auditorium, behind Mike and Monika.

Dr Mose Durst, president of the Unification Church in America, greeted everyone before the ceremony began.

"The family is the core and the heart of a God-centered world..."

There were prayers and proclamations and the taking of vows.

"Do you swear to...."

And the answer was a resounding, "Yes!"

It did cross my mind that I was about to marry a man I had met only one week ago. Yet I reminded myself that this event was much bigger than us and I had to put it all in God's hands.

God's capable hands...then I noticed Bob's hands trembling slightly as he removed his gloves for the exchanging of the Blessing rings. We took out the coveted gold rings and placed them on each other's right ring finger.

There were speeches of congratulations from visiting dignitaries and finally three cheers of "Mansei!" which in Korean means something like "Victory for ten thousand years!" just as around that number of balloons descended from the ceiling upon the giant wedding party.

We were married! But not merely married, we were blessed! The original blessing intended for the first ancestors had been given to us. We were the largest wedding in history and we were dedicating our marriages to world peace. We would strive to be peace-loving global citizens and raise our future children to do the same.

It was a moment of rebirth and an encounter with God and destiny.

Like the man said, it was nice. It was beautiful.

With as much fervor as other world religions stress celibacy as a means to a godly life, Mr. Moon writes that marriage is necessary to complete one's godly duty of seeking perfection in individual and communal life...

(In) the opinion of Rev. Joseph H. Fichter, a Jesuit priest...the Unification theology of marriage might parallel the Roman Catholic concept of 'having a vocation' to the priesthood...—**Charles Austin, in *The New York Times* Metropolitan Report, Friday July 2, 1982.**

22 - KIDNAP OR RESCUE

Myna Bird #1: *When these "de-programmers" seize young Moonies it's not kidnapping.*
Myna Bird #2: *Heavens no. For it to be kidnapping, you have to be an Anglican or something.*
—*Auckland Star* cartoon, August 1983

Is it a kidnapping or rescue when families take back their adult children and hide them from the Moonies?...Auckland lawyer and Council for Civil Liberties member Dr. Rodney Harrison says the question is a complex one which he will ask the Council to investigate...The Moonies are upset that the police are not trying to find Miss Ryan...(but)..Detective Inspector Gerry Hugglestone said today: 'I will not be railroaded into launching a police inquiry by cult members who have lost one of their disciples.'

Dr Harrison said today the issue...raised apparent civil liberties issues on both sides. The first question the council would need to consider was the validity of claims that the Moonies used brainwashing techniques to recruit and keep members.

Auckland Star's *Backgrounder* column, August 9.

***

Tuesday, August 9, 1983

Early in the morning, Bridget Gardner left her parents' home in the exclusive suburb of Epsom, a little south of Parnell, and got into her car. As she drove off, she had no idea that a dark-haired man was following her.

He kept her in his sight across the Auckland Harbor Bridge and as she continued to travel north on the northern motorway. Traffic was heavy with morning commuters and as he reached a stretch of motorway somewhere near the Hibiscus Coast Highway, she was gone. She must have exited the motorway, he realized, but where? Which exit? He had no idea.

An hour later, back at his office, he called Chris at the church. "I lost her," he said. "Sorry. I'll try again tomorrow."

***

Ever since that night when he heard that Maree had been taken, Warren could not shake the conviction that she was somewhere in Whangaparaoa. Even while he'd been busy at work, never mentioning the idea to anyone, the feeling kept nagging at him that he needed to act on his inspiration.

On Monday at the airport, when Warren reported for work as usual, his manager could see there was something on his mind. In all his years at Air New Zealand, the older man could hardly recall an employee as valuable as Warren; he was patient, honest, dependable and meticulous to a fault.

The manager knew Warren attended the church in Parnell that people called the Moonies. If they were all like Warren, it had to be a better church than most, he reckoned. Yet, the papers were not kind to them. He'd seen the articles in the *Herald* about the missing girl. The police weren't even sympathetic. That had to be hard.

Later in the day after much consideration, he took Warren aside. "You may as well be there with your people. Take some time off."

The following day, Warren went to the church center in Parnell and reported to Sarah.

"The boss said I could take some time off to be with 'my people,' so here I am."

"That's wonderful, Warren. You're welcome to stay here for a few days. Hopefully you can be a stabilizing influence on the members. It's been a bit chaotic."

Grinning at the implied compliment, Warren sensed this might be a good time to bring up his inspiration, insight or whatever it was.

He offered it tentatively, trying to strike the right balance between confidence and humility. He knew he had a gift, yet from prior experience, he'd learned to be careful in presenting spiritual insights to other people.

By her expression he could see that Sarah took it seriously.

"Usually your intuition is good, and I trust it. This inspiration also happens to coincide with what the psychic lady said."

Warren's brown eyes widened. He hadn't heard about the spiritualist's visit.

"She had a strong feeling that Maree is somewhere near the sea, facing North. I think Whangaparaoa is one of the places that fits the description. Isn't that right, Chris?" Chris, who was passing by them in the hallway, nodded in confirmation.

Warren was encouraged. Pieces of the puzzle were starting to click into place. At least *some* pieces.

"A trip up to the Whangaparaoa region might be a good idea. Perhaps someone might like to go with you? I know Peter is eager to get involved in some way."

Warren and Peter were good friends, frequently working on church vehicles together. Both were practical, yet spiritual. Peter eagerly accepted the invitation, and after he'd finished his immediate task of changing the oil on the church's truck, the two set off on their journey.

As they drew closer to the peninsula, Warren explained more to Peter about where they were going.

"I'd like to check out the Peter Snell Youth Village. Grant said he had a 'feeling' about it, and it fits with what I received about Whangaparaoa."

"What exactly is the Peter Snell Village?"

"It's a residential youth campsite, and it's on the peninsula, at 1212 Whangaparaoa Road."

Warren had done some research in advance and held out a map of the area. Peter took the pieces of paper.

"I see, very interesting. It overlooks the sea, to the north. There's even a walking track to the beach. Sounds like a nice place."

"Nice place to hide, possibly."

"Yeah... You know what I've just noticed on this map?"

"No, what?

"The peninsula sticks out into the ocean, like a mechanical claw... or maybe a deformed crayfish claw."

Warren's eyes widened. "Very interesting."

They stopped on a dead-end street at Army Bay and parked the car, then walked around the Youth Village using flashlights to scan the area. But it was getting dark and they were unfamiliar with the place.

Warren felt desperate to try and connect to the spirit world. They'd helped him before. Would they help now?

"Where are you? What am I looking for?"

But there was no answer that he was aware of. There was no sign of any activity and no sign of Maree.

Unknown to them, the beach house where Maree was being held was only a short distance away. They were so close! Yet, due to the mysterious workings of the cosmos, or perhaps human limitations (who knows?), they were not able to locate her on that Tuesday night, despite their earnest efforts.

Disappointed, Warren drove Peter back to Parnell.

23 - "FAT MAREE"

A prisoner cannot enter into contracts.
—Nelson Mandela

Tuesday, August 9, 1983

I ate nothing at all, the whole day. They continued offering me meals, which I refused, but other than that, they left me alone. The peace and quiet was wonderfully restorative, better than food. I drank a little water and reflected over many things, including the complicated relationship I'd had with food for much of my life.

I could still remember my teens. I was fat and miserable. One time I went on a diet for a week. I'd tried so hard all week to keep my daily calories to 1000. At end of week, I weighed myself on the bathroom scale. No change! The disappointment was more than I could bear. Feeling helpless and hopeless, I immediately ate three pieces of toast with butter and rhubarb jam.

Mum was thin, and openly admired other thin women, like Grace Kelly, Jackie Kennedy and Audrey Hepburn. The ideal woman was tall, slim and pretty. Mum had such high hopes for me when I was a child. "You have high cheekbones and a long neck. You could be like Audrey Hepburn."

In the 1970s, the ideal female figure was 34-24-34. Thirty-four-inch bust, twenty-four-inch waist, thirty-four-inch hips. Thighs should be 16 inches around. My sisters and I would check ourselves with a tape measure to see how close we were. We knew girls who had those perfect dimensions and we were in awe of them.

As a skinny, awkward twelve-year-old, I could imagine achieving the feminine dream-body, but as I entered my teens, the dream slipped further and further out of my grasp. I blame puberty, but also the bike accident.

When I was 13, I rode my bicycle home from Saturday youth orchestra practice, grasping the handle of my violin case in my right hand, along with the bike handle. The narrow end of the case dangled close to the spokes of my front wheel, but I didn't notice, too busy day-dreaming about the boy in the front row of the first violins. I idolized him, yet he never noticed me. *But what if, someday...?*

Then *bam!* The violin case had gotten stuck in my front wheel and I lost control of my bike, landing hard on the asphalt road. The impulse to throw out my arms to break the fall caused me to break my wrist.

Six weeks in a cast, I took the bus to school, and without the daily bike ride that was my main source of regular exercise, I gained pounds, twenty or more, enough to change my body and my life. At 14, one of my friends gave me a new nickname: "Fat Maree."

"You used to be skinny," said a classmate.

"You used to be pretty," said another.

"I'd hate to go out with a girl like you," said my brother, who was usually nice.

"You've put on the beef!" said Uncle Mick.

"Are you watching your figure?" asked Sister Angela, who'd been my teacher when I was thin.

"You should go on a diet," said my sisters. *"Fatty!"*

"Don't be mean," Mum scolded, then served me an extra-large helping of boiled cabbage. "Good for dieters!"

I did go on diets, but they didn't help. I tried doing exercises from an army book called 5BX, but that didn't make any difference.

"You're getting fatter and fatter," said my father from his recliner one Saturday night, after too many beers.

What was a plump teenager to do? I knew I'd never be Audrey Hepburn. I had the long neck but that's where the resemblance ended. I felt hideous from the neck down. I was deeply ashamed of my stooping shoulders, droopy breasts, bulging belly, large hips and ugly legs. My sister's legs were brown and shapely from playing basketball and tennis and lying out in the sun. Mine were white, flabby and dimpled. I used to wish I could cut myself off at the neck, but that would be dumb, because then I'd be dead.

I grew increasingly depressed and ate compulsively. Food became my solace, even though it was also my enemy and my undoing. I remember waking in the mornings, feeling that I had absolutely nothing to look forward to, except for three things: breakfast, lunch and dinner. The rest of my day looked bleak and miserable.

"I should take you to the doctor," said Mum, exasperated. "There must be something *wrong* with you." I didn't want to go. It was too embarrassing.

"None of the girls at work are like you." I knew what she meant. None of them were as *fat* as me. I felt my shame and frustration burst into a hot flame of anger as I spat out my next words.

"You don't care about me, you just don't like having a fat daughter!"

That was Mum's opportunity to be kind, reassuring and unconditional. But instead she said something that cut me to the core.

"That's right, I *hate* having a fat daughter!"

It wasn't a confession or an apology, more like a declaration of war. She was ashamed of me, embarrassed, and I was crushed. My 16-year-old mind wrestled with the shock of this new information, wondering if my mother even loved me at all, the *real* me that was still there, underneath all the fat, the part of me that was sad, frightened and bewildered, betrayed by my own body. I needed some word or gesture of understanding and compassion which my thin mother seemed unable to give.

***

Then I thought about the words Mum had said to me in the car that night: "Maree, we're doing this for your own good."

What did that mean? I was leading a healthy, fulfilling life. Sure, I'd dropped out of school, but then I'd completed my B.A. degree by correspondence while living in the Sydney church center. I wasn't doing drugs or any self-destructive behavior. I had a decent man in my life and the prospect of starting a family with him. Wasn't that what most parents wished for their children? Why would she want to interfere with my happiness?

What if this was another situation where Mum simply couldn't stand the embarrassment? What if she was actually thinking and feeling on some level, conscious or subconscious, "I *hate* having a Moonie daughter"?

Was this whole abomination more about her own good than mine?

24 - PARABLE OF THE SEEDS

Can you follow your beloved? Can you forget the words of promise? Can you go over the hill which you believe impossible to cross?
—Hyo Won Eu, Unification Church President, early 1960s

Wednesday, August 10, 1983

I woke in the early hours of the morning while it was still dark, feeling famished. I had eaten nothing since Monday at breakfast. I could read my watch by the light coming through the top of the window; whether it was moonlight, starlight or streetlight, I couldn't tell. But I could read the time, which was 2 am, and that meant my forty hours fast was over.

Someone had left a glass of juice by the bed. After a brief prayer I picked it up and drank the whole thing; it tasted divine. Then I sank back into a peaceful sleep.

***

Everyone seemed relieved when I ate the breakfast cereal they brought me.

Afterward, Joe Junior announced that we would be doing a group study of Lifton. John, Mary and others would join us.

"What's Lifton?" I wondered. In reply, Joe held up a thick hard-cover textbook.

"It's a book. *Thought Reform and the Psychology of Totalism* by Robert Jay Lifton. It's the standard study of thought-reform techniques used on prisoners of war in North Korea and China. We won't study the entire thing, only Chapter 22, *Ideological Totalism.*"

It sounded intimidating and I braced myself internally.

"In Chapter 22, he outlines the main psychological themes that are central to the process of thought reform. He calls them the Eight Steps of Mind Control."

I tried not to roll my eyes.

We each had a copy of the book to look at. I sat on the bed with mine. Others made themselves comfortable on the floor, backs to the wall, Joe Junior in charge. We examined the chapter line by line, taking turns to read aloud a few paragraphs at a time. Occasionally someone would offer an earnest comment when they read something which seemed to resonate with their personal experiences or observations. It almost felt like a Christian Bible study.

Step One of Mind Control is called Milieu Control. According to Lifton, to brainwash someone you control everything they see, hear, express or experience. Even one's attitude toward oneself is controlled. Both the external and the "internal environment" are controlled by outside forces. A process he calls "personal closure" takes place as the individual ceases searching for truth.

I could see what was happening here. I was supposed to recognize the Unification Church in this description, but in fact, I could not recall experiencing anything like "personal closure" in the church. Continuous learning and personal growth were expected and encouraged. External control was not something I related to either. In the church I was free to leave at any time, but I stayed, because I *wanted* to.

Yet the concept of being controlled had a familiar ring to it because *right now*, *right here,* I was experiencing something resembling milieu control. I had no freedom here, I could not leave even though I wanted to; internally, they were seeking to control my attitudes and belief system. I had no access to the outside world, no way to check facts or seek alternative opinions. I realized a crucial point:

Deprogramming is a kind of thought control. Yet they try and deflect the blame for it by accusing other groups of the very thing they do themselves.

We moved on to Step Two, Mystical Manipulation, a process by which "controllers" promote specific patterns of behavior and emotion within the group. Serving a higher purpose is stressed. The organization is said to be chosen by God or history to fulfill a mystical imperative such as a great and noble historical goal...

Instantly, several solid rebuttals presented themselves.

What's wrong with a higher purpose? or with noble goals? The Israelites under Moses had a noble goal of escaping from Egypt back to the Promised Land. The disciples of Jesus and St Paul were called to save souls and build God's kingdom. What would Joe Alexander have said about Moses speaking with God in the burning bush? Or Saul's conversion on the road to Damascus? He would have called them deranged lunatics, and their followers would be victims of Mystical Manipulation...he would have had them all hauled off for deprogramming!

What would they have me do? Abandon my ideals and simply live a life devoted to myself? I didn't want that. A self-centered life would be small and insignificant and hardly worth living.

The others expressed more agreeable opinions.

John said, "Yeah, I can really relate to that Mystical Manipulation stuff. In the church if you're not serving a higher purpose you get judged for being selfish."

"Yes," agreed Rosalind, but in a kinder tone. "There is definitely that pressure to live for 'the purpose of the whole.'"

"Right," said Mary. "Moon and his underlings know how to manipulate you into being subordinated to this higher purpose, and you feel like there's no way out."

"Yep. Then you're nothing but a pawn in the hands of the organization," added John.

I said nothing. I could not relate to their terribly cynical interpretation of a movement I had come to know and love. Their negativity saddened me.

Bridget arrived and joined the discussion.

"I used to believe that Koreans were the Chosen People," she told us, "but after visiting Seoul and realizing it had multiple red-light districts, I became disillusioned."

Bridget, you silly person! Ancient Israel had prostitutes, and it didn't stop them from being the Chosen People.

Silly or not, the more they shared, the more I felt uneasy. I started doubting myself and wondering, if the church is as good as I think it is, why do so many people leave? Why did everyone in this room, except me, succumb to a few days of deprogramming? They weren't bad people. Rosalind especially seemed rather nice. Was it possible that they were right, and I was just too proud or too stubborn to see it their way?

***

After lunch I learned that I would be allowed to go outside. A group of us walked across the street and down to a sandy beach that curved gracefully around the edge of an ocean bay. The water was a grayish color, reflecting the August sky. There was a brisk, wintry breeze. I heard gulls and the comforting sound of the sea. Along the shore, we walked through rocks, shells, seaweed and pieces of driftwood.

It felt like a miracle to be out of the stale atmosphere of the drab, crowded house. Whether this was a reward for good behavior I had no idea. I greedily inhaled the fresh, ocean-scented air.

***

Another surprise awaited me later in the evening. Someone had called a doctor to examine me, perhaps to check for any adverse medical conditions arising from my two days of fasting. As the doctor poked, prodded and probed me in full view of everyone out in the front room, I wondered if I could somehow send him an S.O.S., raise the alarm and let him know I was a prisoner.

My heart was racing, and I knew I had to think fast. If I blurted out, "Help! These people kidnapped me and they're keeping me here against my will!" would I sound paranoid and delusional? They believed I was a victim of mind control. Had they told him I had mental problems? If I came across as a crazy person would he put me in an institution? A hand-written note slipped discreetly to the doctor might be less dramatic and more convincing, but I had no paper or writing tools. While I was still trying to figure out my best strategy, the doctor announced I was in good health and began packing up his equipment. He left while I was still paralyzed by indecision.

Afterward, I couldn't help feeling that I had missed out on an opportunity.

***

That night we watched a documentary, *Thy Will be Done*, based on the Moore Report, an examination of new religious organizations and "cults" in America. It started with a terrifying scene of horror in the jungles of South America... Jonestown. Later it showed interviews with former members of various groups, including the Unification Church.

The film was disturbing and made me anxious. I retired for the night, thrown off balance and still bewildered about the overwhelming numbers of ex-members.

"Why do so many leave?" I asked God, the universe or whoever might be listening. I prayed, then opened the Bible. It opened at the parable of the sower and the seeds in the Gospel of Matthew.

"Some seed fell along the path, and the birds came and devoured it. Other seed fell on rocky ground, where it had not much soil, and immediately it sprang up, since it had no depth of soil; and when the sun rose it was scorched, and since it had no root it withered away. Other seed fell among thorns and the thorns grew up and choked it, and it yielded no grain. And other seeds fell into good soil and brought forth grain, growing up and increasing and yielding thirtyfold and sixtyfold and a hundredfold."

It was exactly what I needed.

25 - MARGARET

In prayer it is better to have a heart
without words than words without a heart.
—Mahatma Gandhi

Wednesday, August 10, 1983

Once again Bridget Gardner left her home early in the morning and was discreetly followed by a tall dark man in a car. This time he was able to spot which exit she used when leaving the northern motorway. It was Whangaparaoa Road.

"Yessss, got you this time."

She was far enough ahead of him to have parked and exited her car before he located it and made a positive identification based on the license plate number. He waited a while, watching for signs of activity around any of the houses on the block since he hadn't been able to spot which house she had gone into.

"Where are you? Which one is it?"

The houses were on larger lots than city homes, but still, she could have gone into any one of half a dozen that were near where she parked. The neighborhood was quiet, nothing much going on.

Later he reported to Chris:

"I've found the neighborhood. Tomorrow I should know the exact address. We're getting close."

"Good man," said Chris.

***

The community of members at Parnell was a close-knit group in which people felt a strong empathy with one another. How outrageous that someone would just "snatch" one of them and subject them to Lord-knows-what kind of an ordeal! How disappointing that anyone's parents would support and condone such a thing! Everyone was devastated by the situation but perhaps none more so than Margaret.

Margaret was close to Maree. They were both musical and sometimes sang together, Maree adding alto harmonies to Margaret's pure, sweet soprano voice, Margaret often accompanying with her skillful guitar playing. She was a gentle soul with a tender heart.

When Maree was first kidnapped, Margaret felt that the best and possibly the only thing she could do to help was to pray. Day after day, she went to the prayer room to pray and sing; that would be her contribution. Sometimes she could feel so connected with Maree in her prayer, it was as though she was *there* with Maree, wherever "there" was.

Margaret's older sister Jenny had joined the Unification Church many years earlier. When their mother Gillian decided to investigate Jenny's new church, she brought Margaret along as well. They attended an International Dinner together, after which Margaret attended a weekend workshop. At the time, Margaret had had some personal difficulties in her life and was praying for guidance. The workshop was an answer to her prayer and she decided to join the church as well. Gillian became an associate or part-time member and was always supportive of both daughters as well as the other members.

On Wednesday Margaret was in the prayer room as usual. Suddenly she could see a beach. It wasn't a dream; she was wide awake. Then she saw Maree walking along the beach. It was so clear, so real. Even clearer was the overwhelming feeling that everything was going to be all right.

Later she shared the vision with some of the others at dinner.

"I saw Maree walking along a beach! She felt free; free inside her heart. I think she's going to be okay. Her spirit is free, I felt it...but I wonder what beach that was."

Warren smiled.

"It's probably one of the beaches in Whangaparaoa."

26 - THE DEMAND FOR PURITY

Attempts to deprogram Moonie Maree Ryan are progressing satisfactorily, her family said today...

'Mum said the longest time it takes is 10 days to two weeks,'
—Miss Ryan's brother Paul (23) said.
***Auckland Star*, Thursday**

Thursday, August 11, 1983

Across the narrow hallway from my room was a large bathroom, containing a toilet, shower and tub. I got ready to take a shower, monitored by the ever-present Mary, who sat on the edge of the bathtub while I disrobed. After placing my clothing on a chair and my jewelry— watch, rings and a gold locket— on a nearby ledge, I stepped into the shower cubicle and thought about the day ahead, as the cool water washed over me.

I've almost been here a whole week. How much longer will I have to stay? Will anyone come for me? Can I hold up under the pressure?

Afterward, I dressed again, in the same clothes I'd been wearing for a week.

Back in the room, I found a cheerful Joe Senior. *Must be Good Cop Day here at Deprogramming Central.*

As we chatted, Joe was staring at my hands.

"You're not wearing your rings! That usually means something."

Looking down at my naked fingers, I realized I had put my watch and locket back on but had accidentally left the rings on the ledge by the bathtub. Joe then launched into a story about some other woman they had captured, who one day stopped wearing her Blessing ring.

"*That* was the turning point, the sign that we'd finally gotten through to her. I think today is a special day."

I think this is called wishful thinking, you silly man!

He smiled benevolently, looking so hopeful that I didn't like to disappoint him.

Sure, if it makes you happy, I'll just leave those rings off and let you guys think whatever you want.

It was easier than that breakdown act I hadn't been able to pull off.

***

We continued to study Lifton for the entire day, with short breaks for meals. Once again, my little cell became a classroom, with five or more students occupying places on the floor. I sat on the bed while Joe Junior took the chair. Number Three of the Eight Steps was The Demand for Purity, and Joe was lecturing. It was about ideological purity, and he was in his element.

"The brainwashing victim is taught to see the world as absolutely good and absolutely evil..."

As he rambled through the dull content, we followed along in our text books.

"Whatever is in accordance with the totalist ideology is good...there's no gray area. They're taught that an ideal state, like a Workers' Paradise, or the Kingdom of Heaven, is attainable, and anything done in its name is ultimately moral...However, the ideal state isn't possible, it's totally alien to the human condition."

Wow.

I hoped Joe didn't notice me rolling my eyes. I needed to be on my best behavior to support Joe Senior's missing ring theory.

What a depressing view of life!

No matter what they told me, I still believed in a benevolent deity, the perfectibility of the human spirit and the real possibility of an earthly Utopia. Didn't Jesus pray for God's will to be done on earth, as it is in heaven? Didn't he say, 'You must be perfect as your heavenly Father is perfect'? Even if I didn't understand what that meant, *he* must have believed in an ideal state.

Optimism and idealism help you get up every day, feeling that life is worth living. I wondered how people like Lifton, or like Joe, could live with their gloomy, hopeless outlook.

I guessed what Joe wanted me to think. He would want me to recognize the Unification Church in that whole whacko description of the sharply divided worlds of good and evil. He would want me to say that my church taught us that *it* was good and everything else was bad.

But I held back. I wouldn't attempt phony denunciations of my faith. Nor would I fight and argue. I would keep my thoughts to myself while trying to analyze and challenge all this information. That would be my strategy from that day forward. In a way, I became two different people. Externally, I was the subdued "deprogramming" victim, minus her rings, submissively studying the Lifton Bible; inwardly I was a warrior, sustaining a spiritual battle for my faith and my soul.

Even if some of my insights were compelling and would have made for a lively discussion, I didn't reveal them. It would be like throwing "pearls before swine" —offering wisdom to people with no appreciation for its value. And I needed these swine to think I was seeing things their way.

Step Four was The Cult of Confession. Confession of past sins was a psychological technique to make people more vulnerable.

Blah blah blah. Sure, maybe this happened to prisoners of war, but it didn't happen to me.

As if knowing my thoughts, Joe explained how this applied to the Unification Church.

"In the Oakland family, members were pushed to share details of their past lives. At the weekend workshops in Boonville, members were 'planted' in discussion groups, to stimulate deep sharing."

I was tired of hearing about Oakland. Perhaps the church there was a tad overzealous. However, I'd never been there, and my experience had been entirely different. I had tried to explain that to my parents and family over the years, but they didn't seem to understand.

The others in the room offered appropriate responses.

"Yeah," said John, "by confessing to everyone, it makes you judge yourself."

"And then you think you have the right to judge others," added Mary.

Good grief. Teacher's pets, every one of them.

They treated Lifton like holy scripture. They were baby birds, open-mouthed and swallowing Mother's worms unquestioningly. Were they incapable of independent thinking? They seemed more brainwashed than I felt.

The demand for purity was strong.

Next was Step Five, The Sacred Science.

Joe was reading aloud from the fat book.

"The totalist organization creates an aura of sacredness around its basic dogma, holding it out to be the ultimate moral vision..."

I could see sunshine through the top of the window. The sky was blue. I wished I wasn't stuck in this room.

"... It is absolutely prohibited to question the basic assumptions of the dogma; reverence is demanded for the originators of this dogma and for the dogma itself. Anyone who opposes it is said to be immoral and unscientific. The controller's dogma is an absolute body of moral principles, true for all men at all times."

I could feel my heart racing and fear rising, while straining to assume an air of nonchalance or at best, mild interest. It sounded so much like *Divine Principle*, I had to think hard.

Reverence was never demanded, was it? Questioning wasn't strictly prohibited, was it? We didn't harshly judge people who opposed the Principle... did we?

Twin serpents of doubt and fear squirmed inside my belly.

Joe read on.

"The 'Sacred Science' offers comfort and security to the individual, unites the mystical and logical, has sweeping insights and gives an extremely intense feeling of truth."

I was confused. Unifying mystical and logical, offering comfort and security: weren't those *good* things? Then why was Joe making them sound so *scary*?

He continued.

"The dogma has a strong hold over a person's mental processes. If someone feels attracted to ideas which contradict or deny or ignore the dogma, he feels guilty or afraid, and therefore his quest for knowledge becomes hampered."

John, former member and night watchman, concurred.

"Yeah, I remember feeling doubts about the *Principle*, but I was too afraid to question anything, so I kept it to myself. I kept on fund-raising for months, probably years, without really believing in what I was doing. I can't believe I wasted all that time."

This was the same John who said he'd never actually read the *Divine Principle*...so he was doubting something he didn't even know. *How was that even possible?* I had to ask.

I did my best to use a friendly, non-confrontational tone. "Why didn't you read the *Principle* to try and answer your own questions?"

Joe thought he had the answer to that one, right there in Lifton. "'When the quest for knowledge becomes hampered, the individual feels afraid to examine other sources of information. Personal closure occurs. The individual feels such a commitment toward the Sacred Science, he either adheres to it totally or just *pretends* to adhere to it even while inwardly resisting.'"

"That sounds like me," said John. "I pretended for a long time."

"Me too," confessed Rosalind. "I pretended to be happy even when I wasn't."

How sad.

If the *Divine Principle* turned out to be some Sacred Science that a sinister controller was employing to manipulate me, I would have to give it up. I didn't want to suffer 'personal closure'. I didn't want my quest for knowledge to be hampered. Why would anyone want that?

But if Joe and company would take away my 'Sacred Science' what would be left?

I inwardly screamed.

I need something to believe in! Doesn't everybody? Please don't take it away!

That night I opened the Bible, desperately seeking answers, but nothing seemed to make any sense.

Mum said it was going fairly well. Maree is fine and quite happy, but I don't think they've had any final successes yet.

—Paul Ryan (23) to the *Auckland Star.*

27 - DOUBLE AGENT

Is my gloom, after all, shade of His hand outstretched caressingly?
—Francis Thompson

Thursday, August 11, 1983

Upstairs in the Parnell center, Peter was busy composing a letter intended for the Opinion Page of the Auckland Star. It began:

I am a Moonie and I love it. Proud to be included in the ranks of those who follow the Rev. Moon, come what may.

Have I rejected my family, stopped loving them? Not on your life! How far and how willingly the parents encourage and support their children in their destinies determines how much of the road they travel together...

By early Thursday, the P.I. had been able to confirm the exact location of the house in which the deprogramming was assumed to be taking place, in other words, the place Bridget Gardner was driving to every day. Mid-morning, Sarah, Pam and Chris met together in Pam's small office.

They now had an address to which they believed Maree had been taken. But would that be enough information to convince the police to act? Sarah reasoned, realistically, that it would not, and carefully explained her thoughts to the others.

"Just because Bridget is going there, doesn't mean something illegal is going on inside the house."

"Right." Chris agreed. "We can't *prove* she's over there helping the deprogrammers."

"She could be going there for some purely innocent reason, like visiting a relative."

"Or feeding a cat."

Pam laughed. "Feeding a *cat*?"

"Yes, for a friend who might be out of town," explained Chris.

"Right," Pam understood. Sarah continued.

"Exactly. None of us really knows what Bridget's doing once she's inside the bach. We also don't know whether anyone else is in the house at all."

Chris nodded. "Right. And even if other people *are* in the house, it doesn't mean they're doing anything illegal."

"At least that's how the police will see it. Bridget's daily trip to a house in Whangaparaoa does not prove that Maree is being held in that same house, even though *we* might be convinced of that."

"That's how Hugglestone will see it, no doubt," said Chris. "He'll say, 'I believe no offence has been committed,' and all the usual balderdash, until we have concrete proof."

"Precisely. We need more evidence," Sarah went on. "That's why I'm thinking of asking David Meek."

"Asking him what, exactly?"

"I know he's friendly with Bridget. I could ask him if he wants to be a kind of double agent."

Chris and Pam both smiled broadly at Sarah's idea.

"Brilliant," said Chris. "So, we get him to fake that he wants to help out at the deprogramming?"

"Yes, and while he's there he can record, or take mental notes of who's there and what's going on."

"Right, and that gives us an eye witness!"

"Fantastic idea! Would you like me to phone him right now?" asked Pam.

"Yes, please," said Sarah.

***

Highly intelligent but on the shy side, David Meek wore a pair of eyeglasses with the kind of thick lenses that people call "Coke-bottle". He liked the church, had thought about joining, but found the lifestyle to be too demanding. He had been living in the Parnell center for several months but had moved out and was preparing to go back to England, where he was from. Because he was on his way out, in a manner of speaking, he could reasonably present himself as an ex-member or opponent of the church. When Meek answered Pam's call, he was genuinely thrilled at the opportunity to help.

"Sure, I'd love to do something." He chuckled a little, anticipating the adventure. "Let me get in touch with Bridget and see if I can get myself an invitation."

28 - "THEY'VE FOUND HER!"

Any kind of prejudice must be eradicated...The world is but one country. People are but one family.
—Baha'i Faith

Friday, August 12, 1983

On Friday, the Auckland Star printed a Letter to the Editor, by a Terence W. Brown of Epsom:

A senior police officer has publicly accused the Unification Church of wasting police time with its request for urgent investigation of the possible kidnapping of church member Maree Ryan.

The officer concerned seems to ignore the fact that the police have a public responsibility to uphold the law regardless of any religious implications involved.

I know little about the Unification Church and its teachings, but whatever they are, the church is entitled to have the complaint honestly and quickly investigated to determine if the 26-year-old woman is being held by her family against her own will. In no circumstances does a family or person have the right to forcibly hold another person.

It should not be difficult for police to locate the woman, as her father has admitted that he has knowledge of the situation.

***

David Meek got his invitation to go with his friend Bridget on Friday to the house where she was assisting in a deprogramming. Bridget introduced him to three Americans as well as several ex-members. She also introduced him to Maree's mother and brother. He did not enter the room where the attempted deprogramming was taking place but was permitted to listen from the hallway. He recognized Maree's voice.

Later he called Sarah at the church and reported everything. Sarah then shared the good news with Chris and Pam.

***

On Friday afternoon, at the offices of Johnston, Prichard and Fee, Martin Knapp received a letter from Bryan Gibson, Assistant Police Commissioner, in response to the one he had sent earlier in the week. It read, in part,

I fully understand the concern of your clients and can assure you that the welfare of Miss Ryan is foremost in the minds of the police. It must be remembered, however, that Miss Ryan is with her mother and brother, and it is the police view that nothing sinister is likely to be done to her in those circumstances.

Knapp sighed. He'd done his best to try to convince the police to enforce the law without prejudice; but it seemed they were stubbornly attached to preconceived notions of the Unification Church. *The thin edge of the wedge...*

At 5 o'clock, he was almost ready to leave his office when the phone rang.

"They've found her!" It was Chris, who then went on to explain about the help from the P.I. as well as David Meek.

"This is wonderful news. I will personally contact the police again."

***

Chris brought Pam up to speed on the latest developments, ending with the fact that Martin Knapp would be talking to the police to discuss the next steps.

"They listen to him!" she exclaimed, exasperated. "Why do they never listen to us?"

29 - LOADING THE LANGUAGE

Perhaps the harassment and vile methods of the 'deprogrammers' (recently seen on television) may soon begin to take their emotional toll on Miss Ryan and re-convert her by family-supported intimidation. Are the police waiting until Miss Ryan is emotionally defeated and no longer willing to state that she has been forcibly held? A dangerous precedent is being set.
—Terence W. Brown, Epsom (to editor of *Auckland Star*)

Friday, August 12, 1983

As we continued studying the Lifton book, I had to admit it was impressive as an academic thesis. Compared to Joe's harangues of the first few days, when his vocabulary seemed limited to a few choice insults, Lifton almost made him seem intelligent.

Once again, we gathered in the small bedroom with our copies of the thick textbook, which was fat enough to be a Bible. I might have referred to it as the "Sacred Science" except that I was trying to be on my best behavior.

I had rescued my rings from the bathroom the previous evening and now kept them in the pocket of my dress.

Today's lesson was Loading the Language. In a totalist environment, you are encouraged to use brief, easily-memorized phrases known as "thought-terminating clichés". This causes the user of such phrases to over-simplify situations or feelings while overlooking the deeper complexities of human nature.

Some examples of thought-terminating clichés in a communist environment might include: *imperialist aggression, bourgeois mentality, proletarian standpoint* and so on.

"So," said Joe, stroking his dark moustache with one hand while holding the book on his lap with the other, "what examples can you all think of, that might be the special clichés of the Moon cult?"

"Well, there's spaced-out, off-center and Satanic," said John, causing an outburst of nervous laughter from the rest of us. We were all familiar with these terms.

"Chapter Two problem!" offered Rosalind. (Chapter Two was the section of Divine Principle that deals with the human fall. A "chapter two problem" could indicate a range of sexual problems such as lust or illicit intercourse.)

"Positive, negative, subject, object, Cain, Abel," Mary contributed, from her spot on the floor where she usually slept. She was still wearing black and as inscrutable as ever.

"Um, possessed?" I suggested, trying to sound like a good student.

Joe approved of the class's progress.

"Yes, the Moonies typically use this language of non-thought. It's an all-encompassing jargon that's relentlessly judgmental. The effect of specialized language is to constrict individuals until they're linguistically deprived. Think about it! Language is so central to the human experience. By restricting your use of language, your capacity for thinking and feeling is immensely narrowed."

Nothing wrong with my capacity for thinking and feeling. I resented the insinuations.

"I can really relate to this next part," Rosalind contributed, "where it says that at first the loading of the language creates insight and security, but eventually causes uneasiness and you retreat into 'rigid orthodoxy'... it was very much like that for me. I really got into all the jargon because I wanted to look good, but there was a deeper part of me that felt, I don't know, like I wasn't being authentic."

Joe was validated, triumphant.

"Because you were *not* being authentic! And the danger is, it says right here, you get so chained to these expected clichés that *your imagination may atrophy from disuse.*"

Nothing atrophied about my imagination. I was indignant at the thought of it.

To be fair, it was true that we used jargon in the church. Those terms that John, Mary and Rosalind mentioned were all real. But wouldn't that be true of any organization? Like in the Catholic church...I tried to come up with a mental list of Catholic language...confession, Communion, mortal sin, venial sin, Vatican One, Vatican Two, the Immaculate Conception, indulgences, the Mass. Catholics had their fair share of jargon, but did that make them brainwashed? I didn't think so.

What did seem like a genuine "loading of the language" though, was the jargon of deprogramming.

Yes!

They used the word "cult" as a thought-terminating cliché. Whenever you called some organization a cult you didn't have to respect it or investigate it. They never used the honorific titles for people like Reverend Moon: they just said "Moon" in a disparaging tone of voice. For witnessing they said "recruiting". Fundraising became "begging" or "peddling". Spiritual education became "indoctrination"; church real estate was always a "compound." Church leaders were "totalist administrators" and so on. With such ugly verbal tricks, they twisted holy and respectable things to sound sinister.

Yet, these people seemed to have no idea that they themselves were "loading the language".

The situation was thick with irony. I silently marveled at it.

30 - G.I. JOE

Stockholm Syndrome appears when an abused victim develops a kind of respect and empathy towards their abuser...This syndrome is also called "traumatic bonding" or "victim brainwashing."
—Internet meme.

The greater the power, the more dangerous the abuse.
—Edmund Burke

On Saturday evening, I was permitted to go to the living room. I had been there before to watch mandatory movies, but this time was different. I could just relax and socialize with Rosalind, Bridget, Mary, Joe and anyone else who was there as though we were just a bunch of friends on vacation. I supposed it was a reward for good behavior. Even my brother was there, sitting on the sofa, laughing and chatting with the rest of the group. I was on the brown-carpeted floor not far from Joe Junior, recalling why I never liked 1970s earth-tones. Everything was the color of dirt.

Someone told a funny story about Jerry, the younger brother of Joe. Apparently, his job was to run miscellaneous errands for the team. One day he'd been walking down the road on his way to buy milk, when he was attacked by a large crow which started pecking the top of his head. I laughed along with the others.

Obviously bad karma. Even the creation doesn't like you.

My brother told another story. As it happened, he shared a room with Joe Junior, but Joe had been experiencing nightmares. Sometimes he woke up calling out to his wife, "Pat! Pat!" His wife, Pat, was back home in America, but my brother, whose name also happens to be Pat, would then wake up saying, "What? What's the matter?"

Maybe Joe was so often gruff and grumpy because he couldn't get a decent night's sleep, I couldn't help wondering.

Or was he being spiritually attacked?

In this changed situation, I saw a different side of Joe Junior. He seemed relaxed, even friendly. From a wallet he pulled out some small black-and-white photographs and handed them to me. They showed a younger Joe in military clothing. There was a helicopter and jungle in the background. It was Vietnam, and suddenly I didn't hate him anymore.

Then he took out a bill from his wallet, an American dollar, and started talking about the symbolism on it, the pyramid topped by a triangle with an eye.

"That's the logo of the Illuminati cult."

"Why would that be on the dollar bill?"

He explained how Franklin Roosevelt, a 32nd degree Mason, had been so impressed with the "all-seeing eye of Providence" from the Great Seal, that he wanted it on the dollar bill. Many of the founders of the United States were also Masons, Joe went on. The Illuminati were a mysterious cult with ties to the Masons.

Wow. Who would have imagined there was such symbolism on a dollar bill? It gave me chills, like a scary movie. Then we were distracted by a loud discussion among the group that was seated on the sofa. Pat and a young woman called Geraldine were arguing over the existence of ghosts and angels. Geraldine, a friend of Rosalind, had come to support the deprogramming effort as an observer, and was insisting that angels were *real* to Pat, who was adamant that they were a figment of her imagination. Predictably, Joe took Pat's side. I stayed out of it.

There was a guitar nearby. I picked it up and strummed the chords to one of my favorite Australian folk songs, *Clancy of the Overflow*, from the poem by A.B. Paterson. I started singing and was pleased to find that I still remembered all the words.

Australia. I had so many fond memories of my time there. My thoughts then flew to Mike Treacy and his kidnapping.

What was the advice he gave us? "Promise yourself that, no matter how you feel at the end, you will state the words, 'I have been kidnapped and I am being held against my will.'" That was good advice.

Something weird was happening to me. I was having friendly feelings toward Joe, of all people. Joe, my tormentor and arch-enemy. It was truly disturbing. I needed to get a firm grip on my thoughts and emotions. After I finished the song, I rehearsed Mike's words inside my head, because that was what I would say to the police, if they ever came for me.

I have been kidnapped and I'm being held here against my will. I have been kidnapped and I'm being held against my will. I have been kidnapped...

31 - “GET THOSE SNAKES!”

Never wound a snake; kill it.
—Harriet Tubman.

Saturday August 13, 1983

I could easily round up a bunch of guys and bust her out of there,” said Tai, on the phone to Chris. Chris grinned at the thought of an elite group of former Special Forces members breaking in to the deprogrammers’ hideout. That would be outstanding! The plan had its merits. However, Chris knew Sarah would be dead set against it. She was trying to work through more orthodox channels.

“Thanks for the offer, but I’m pretty sure that’s not how we want to go about it.”

“Okay. But be sure to let me know if you change your mind. I’ve got some boys here that are dying for some action.”

***

Some of the members were also in the mood for action. Peter wanted to stage a protest.

"Now that we know where she is," said Peter, "why don't we go out there with our signs and make a whole lot of noise? We could call the TV people and newspapers."

"No, because then they'll know that we've found them," said Sarah. *We need to take them by surprise.*

"What if some of us try to break in to the house and get her out?" asked Grant. "We could bring baseball bats or something."

"Yeah, a baseball bat to the kneecaps is pretty effective," said Mark, a former rugby player.

"No," said Sarah, "but thank you for your suggestions." *I hope they're joking.*

Warren, who had been staying at the center since early in the week, felt particularly frustrated. If only he could have been more in tune with the situation that night when he was out at the Peter Snell Youth Village. He'd been so close! From the description of the house they had identified in Whangaparaoa, he must have been within a few blocks of where Maree was that very night, perhaps a stone's throw away. He felt so bad that he hadn't been successful and as a result, Maree had been kept for another five days at least.

Sarah was exhausted but was not about to act hastily out of sheer impatience, or under pressure from the members. *They don't understand.*

She fully appreciated the urgency and anxiety of the members, and how, given enough time, deprogrammers were adept at breaking the will and the spirit of their victims. The members were afraid that, by waiting too long to act on the information they had, they might be too late. Sarah felt responsible for the whole situation, including its outcome. As National Leader of the church, this thing had happened on her watch and she was determined to see that it was handled with wisdom and care. Most of all she was concerned for Maree's well-being. *But whatever we do to get her back needs to be safe and legal, otherwise it could just blow up in our faces.*

She was still waiting to hear back from Martin Knapp, who was trying to communicate with his contacts in the upper echelons of the Auckland Police Department. *Ideally, it would be best if Knapp can convince the police to get involved.*

"We'll see what Knapp has to say, and we'll follow his advice," she told everyone, to calm them down. "In the meantime, please keep praying, fasting and offering devotions as you wish. We're getting really close now and it's important that we do things properly. If we start doing crazy stuff it's only going to come back to haunt us later on. You know how people are."

Chris agreed with Sarah, but from a different perspective. Of course, he wanted to rescue Maree, and was concerned about PR, but he also wanted justice. The Alexanders had been "picking off" church members for too long, as if they were an extermination team ridding the world of vermin. But they themselves were the real vermin. It was time for these guys to get what was coming to them. They were already in legal trouble in the U.S., and if they were violating probation, they could be put away for life. Therefore, law enforcement had to be involved.

Chris had been following the American deprogramming skullduggery for so long now, it was a matter of professional pride for him to see these crooks behind bars. They now had a window of opportunity.

"We need to crush them," he said. "We need to get those snakes."

32 - RESCUE

In everyone's life, at some time, our inner fire goes out. It is then burst into flame by an encounter with another human being. We should all be thankful for those people who rekindle the inner spirit.
—***Albert Schweitzer***

Sunday, August 14, 1983
8 am

Warren arrived at the Parnell house, having been summoned by Sarah. Normally people would be setting up chairs, practicing songs and getting everything prepared for the 11 am Sunday Service. But there was no activity downstairs. Something else is going on.

Chris and Geoff were in the hallway looking as if they were ready to go somewhere.

Sarah stepped out of the office. "Okay, we're going. Let's take your car, Warren. All right?"

He led the way to where he'd parked his green Valiant and opened the front passenger door for Sarah while Geoff and Chris got in the back seat.

Sarah gave him an address in Ellerslie and looked so serious that he drove there without asking whose place it was. When they arrived, Sarah, Chris and Geoff got out. Sarah looked at Warren, her expression grave and intensely focused. "We won't be long."

Warren couldn't help noticing a yellow E-type Jaguar in the driveway.

Whoever owns this place has good taste in cars.

Before long, the three re-appeared with a tall man in a sharp-looking three-piece business suit.

That must be Knapp. Warren had heard good things about the church's lawyer.

Sarah came back to the Valiant and got in. Chris bounded over to the Valiant but stopped at the driver's side window. "We're going in the Jag with Knappy!" then headed toward the primrose car.

Warren and Sarah exchanged a look.

"We're going to the police station," Sarah instructed. Warren put the Valiant into reverse to back up out of Knapp's driveway.

***

In my small room at the house near the beach, I woke up.

It's Sunday the 14th. I've been here ten days. Will anyone ever come for me? I could feel my hope starting to fade.

***

8:45 am

At the station, a bland, concrete, multi-storied building on Gray's Avenue in central Auckland, again Warren stayed in the car. He really didn't mind playing chauffeur, he was just glad to be able to help with whatever was going on. Obviously, something big was happening.

Before long, two men came out of the building along with Sarah and Knapp. One was a uniformed policeman of average height and build; the other wore plain clothes and was about as tall as Knapp but heavier. Knapp rejoined the two brothers in the Jaguar. Sarah came back to the Valiant. The police officers got into a third vehicle which was plain and unmarked.

Sarah gave Warren a small piece of paper on which there was an address and a roughly-drawn map. "This is a three-way intersection in Whangaparaoa. We'd like you to lead the way there." *This is it.* Warren felt a surge of excitement and optimism.

He'd sensed all along that they needed to go to Whangaparaoa, he just hadn't been able to pinpoint a location. Now, Sarah had an actual address. This was amazing, miraculous.

***

I stretched and did some exercises while Mary watched.

***

9:00 am

A convoy of three vehicles headed north up the Auckland motorway with Warren's green Valiant in front, followed by the Jaguar driven by Martin Knapp and lastly, the unmarked police car.

The uniformed officer was younger and lower in rank than the other. He was driving.

"So, what do you think about all this Moonie stuff?" he asked the other.

"Doesn't matter what I think, I'm just doing my job."

"Yeah, but really. Everyone has some opinion."

"You got that right. There's a lot of opinion on both sides. Kind of a he said/she said type of thing, like a really bad divorce."

The younger man chuckled. "Never thought of it like that."

"Yeah, so there's the Moonies' side of it, versus everyone else's. Or, the Moonies' side of it, versus Hugglestone's. And the truth might be somewhere in the middle."

"I guess you've got a point. It's not just Hugglestone that can't stand them though. On the force, I mean."

"Really? What are you referring to?"

"Some of the higher-ups like Gibson are downright hostile."

"Is that a fact? What have you heard?" The older man's attentiveness suddenly sharpened at the name. Bryan Gibson was Assistant Police Commissioner.

"Gibson was in Auckland on some official business and he shouted us guys a few rounds of drinks after work. I don't remember how it came up—maybe someone was going through the pub peddling posies or something—and anyway, Gibson goes, 'I have no time for the Moonies.'"

"Hmmm. What else did he say?"

"Said he'd seen them in action overseas and begging on the streets in Wellington. Oh yeah, one of his friends had a son who got hooked up with them. The kid committed suicide."

The other man whistled, then both were silent for a short while. The older man in plain clothes spoke first.

"Doesn't mean it's the Moonies' fault that a kid kills himself. Perhaps he was going to do it anyway."

"Yeah, I s'pose that's possible. Then the Moonies get all the blame."

***

In the green Valiant, there was little conversation. Warren, fully aware of the gravity of his mission, drove up the motorway, ahead of the Jaguar and the police car, following the main road as it snaked through green countryside.

Meanwhile in the front passenger seat of the Jaguar, Chris was in a chatty mood.

"Deprogramming has been called the psychological gang-rape of a victim."

"Goodness." Knapp listened with interest as he drove.

"Some of the great saints experienced something akin to what Maree is going through right now."

"Really, how so?"

"When Thomas Aquinas wanted to join the new Dominican Order at age 19, his mother had him seized by his brothers and held prisoner in a family castle for a year."

"And when was this?"

"1244 A.D."

"Well, well. And yet it sounds eerily familiar."

"Exactly. And Francis of Assisi was imprisoned by his parents who didn't like his new lifestyle as a beggar-monk."

"Goodness gracious. Sounds like Maree's in good company, then."

"Right. Then of course, there was the Spanish Inquisition."

***

Mary brought breakfast. Weet-Bix and milk, in a Styrofoam bowl with the obligatory plastic spoon. Toast, sparsely buttered, with Vegemite. Slowly, I ate my prison food, wondering what the day would hold.

***

10:00 am

Warren parked on the left-hand side of the road before it branched into a fork. He watched as Knapp stopped the Jaguar across the street from him. The officers pulled up behind Warren and the taller one got out.

Warren wound down the driver's side window and could smell the ocean. It was a sunny day but the breeze coming from the sea had a chill to it. The taller officer walked up to Warren's window. He was wearing a sports coat over a shirt and tie. Warren could read the name on his ID tag: Detective Inspector Peter Robinson.

"We'll need you folks to stay here while we go and interview the girl. If she's content to stay with her mother, then that'll be the end of the matter."

Sarah nodded. "Yes, we understand."

Warren and Sarah watched the policemen pull out and drive down the left fork of the forked road.

***

In the Jaguar, Chris and Geoff waited with Martin Knapp. Chris looked across at Knapp. "So, how many do you think they'll arrest? All of them are accessories, including the mother."

Knapp had adjusted the black leather driver's seat to recline and pushed it back far enough to stretch his long legs. His expression was serious, and he spoke slowly.

"There's nothing to stop them from arresting everyone in that house, nothing at all."

Chris looked skeptical. "Where's the SWAT team, then? And the paddy-wagons? How do two officers nab a whole houseful of crooks, without any guns? Shouldn't they have back-up?"

Geoff, stretched out in the back seat, also had his doubts. The police seemed too relaxed.

"If this was Japan, they would've had hordes of Ninjas arriving by night."

Chris chuckled. "Like that scene in *Shogun*, where they attack the castle?"

"Yes. It helps to be able to be invisible."

Chris turned serious again. "We have to get these snakes somehow. These Alexanders need to be put away for life. We have them virtually in our own back yard!" He made fists with his hands as if preparing for a fight.

Knapp was more reserved. "Everything depends on what Maree says when they talk to her. If she's happy where she is, then that's the end of that."

Chris had never stopped believing in Maree. "She's a trooper. No way is she going to stay with those bastards and her mother. She'll be wanting out of there."

"I have a bad feeling, though," said Knapp. "Not about Maree, about the police."

Geoff scoffed from the back seat. “You mean, they don’t know what they’re doing? I’ve noticed that.”

“They only sent two men, and I think I know why.”

Chris and Geoff waited for the answer.

“They don’t expect her to leave.”

***

“I need to take a shower,” I told Mary. She got up from the floor and followed me to the bathroom.

***

10:15 am

“This is the place,” said Detective Inspector Peter Robinson, checking in his notebook for the address which had been given him by Martin Knapp.

“So, we’re going in?”

“Yep, we’re going in.”

***

10:30 am

Geoff was the first to notice the police cruiser as it returned, completed a U-turn, then pulled up behind them. “Looks like we’ve got company.”

Knapp rolled down the driver’s side window as Detective Robinson and his companion approached. “We’ve had a sit-down with the group and it was extremely cordial. They all confirm that it’s nothing more than a family reunion.”

Knapp squinted his eyes and looked up at Robinson. “But what about Maree? What did *she* have to say?”

“She was taking a shower.”

“So, you didn’t speak to her?”

“Correct.”

Knapp sighed, then opened the car door and stood up. At full height, he faced Robinson eye to eye.

“Did you happen to notice any foreigners on the premises?”

"There were a couple of guys that sounded American," said the uniformed officer.

"Those will be your kidnappers and deprogrammers, since Maree doesn't have any American relatives." The detective cleared his throat awkwardly. Knapp went on. "You have to go back there and interview her. *That's why we're here.* Quickly, in case you've already scared them off."

"Right-oh, then, we'll check back over there and see about interviewing the girl." The officers turned to leave, then stopped in their tracks as Knapp spoke again.

"The *girl* is a 26-year-old woman. And I suggest you take Sarah with you, so Maree can have a familiar face to greet her when she gets out."

"Right-oh."

"Go, Knappy!" said Chris in a half-whisper intended for Geoff, as they watched the policemen cross the street to where the Valiant sat.

"That lawyer's a bit of a pit-bull, isn't he?" muttered the junior officer as soon as they were safely out of earshot.

Robinson disagreed. "More like an aggressive greyhound."

***

Warren watched as the two men strode purposefully across the road toward his car. "Okay, they're back, but they don't appear to have her." *What's going on?* He rolled the window down. The detective looked past Warren and spoke to Sarah.

"It appears they tried to call our bluff, but we'll have another go. We think you ought to join us as well, just in case."

Just in case what?

Sarah got out and joined the two policemen, leaving Warren by himself, while sea-gulls circling high above him made a lonely sound.

***

10:45 am

They came for me that Sunday morning. I could hardly believe it was really happening. I'd almost given up hope of ever being found.

I dressed after my shower and returned to my room, when there was a knock on the door. That was strange. *No one ever knocks. They just barge in.*

"The police are here, and they want to talk to you," said Joe Junior. *What? The police?* Joe didn't sound all that worried about the police being there. He must have thought he'd successfully won me over.

A tall, well-built man entered the room. He was not wearing a uniform but a name tag on his sports coat told me he was Detective Inspector Peter Robinson. He said he needed to ask me something.

"Are you here of your own free will?"

"No."

"No?" he sounded surprised.

"I'm being held against my will and I'd like to leave." The words came easily as I'd rehearsed them many times in my mind.

"Well then, I'm here to release you. You're free to come with me." *Free? I'm free?* It almost sounded too good to be true. As the tall man dutifully escorted me out of the room, I felt he was my savior.

Out of that room! As we moved down the hallway toward the living area, I could see sunshine beckoning from the front door, and freedom.

As we passed through the living room, I saw her again: my mother, scared and small like a hunted, bird-like creature, colorful plastic rollers in her tightly wound white hair. She looked so pitiful it took the edge off my need for revenge. Then she made her angry, frowny face.

"I could go to jail for this," she scolded, as if that would be all my fault. *Unbelievable!*

"Don't worry, Mum, I won't press charges," was all I said to her. We didn't touch each other.

But the others were different. Even in my charade of being broken down by them, a strange bond had grown up amongst us. I hugged my brother. I hugged Rosalind, Bridget, even Mary who always dressed in black.

And I hugged Joe, whom I'd hated with a passion, screamed and yelled at, argued with and mocked with every resource at my disposal; because now he was slumped against a porch railing on the front deck looking completely forlorn.

"Thanks, Joe," I said. He hugged back but wouldn't look at my face.

The policeman opened the back door of his car and as I got in, I saw...Sarah. What a relief! I sat down beside her.

"Sorry to be so much trouble," I told her, even though I had no clue.

"No trouble." She smiled warmly, and we sat in silence as the police car took us back through the country roads toward the city.

SOUTHLAND TIMES, August 15, 1983

"Miss Ryan Taken from House" was the headline.

A young woman member of the Unification Church who was allegedly abducted 10 days ago for deprogramming was taken from a Whangaparaoa house by the police yesterday and returned to the church.

The woman, Maree Ryan, last night described from the church headquarters in Parnell how she had been abducted...

Detective Inspector Peter Robinson asked Miss Ryan if she was being held against her will.

"She said she was, and so we had no choice but to release her from where she was being held," Mr. Robinson said.

AUCKLAND STAR, Monday August 15: *"I felt like an animal in a cage."*

Moonie Maree Ryan says she felt like an animal in a cage during 10 days of professional deprogramming organized by her mother.

She said today she was thrilled to be back with 18 other Moonies living in a house in St Stephens Ave, Parnell.

"I know who my real friends are."

Detective Inspector Peter Robinson...said Mrs. Ryan was "not too pleased" when police took her daughter away. Mrs. Ryan was staying with a friend in Auckland today but was out when The Star tried to contact her. The friend said Mrs. Ryan was "brassed off" with earlier reports she considered a pack of lies.

Maree's father said today he did not believe a word the Moonies said, and that his daughter was brainwashed.

"They call themselves a church...it is ridiculous.

"They are good kids, but they are slaves. It is a sort of brain damage. It would take about 12 months to get her back to being a normal person."

Robinson had been told the deprogrammers caught last night's 9:30 flight to Los Angeles.

33 - THE QUEST FOR JUSTICE

It [Deprogramming] should be prosecuted, not just as any other kidnapping undertaken for mercenary motives should be, but even more vigorously, since it strikes at the most precious and vulnerable portion of the victim's life, religious convictions and commitments.
***—Dean Kelley, Director for Religious liberty, National Council of Churches*, USA**

The next few days passed like a dream, as I began adjusting to life outside of my little prison. I recall Sarah taking me for a special outing to some hot pools near Auckland. Afterward, back at the church center, Margaret insisted I lie face down on the floor of the sisters' room, so she could give me a massage. It was wonderful. "I knew you would be okay," she said soothingly, while kneading my shoulders, "as soon as I saw you on the beach that day." A steady stream of reporters came to the church to talk to me and take my picture. It was big news that someone would leave a deprogramming and go back to the church or religion from which their family was so desperate to remove them. I was a novelty and a local celebrity, on TV and in front-page news for about three weeks in that memorable August.

If I went to the bank or the Post Office, invariably someone would recognize me. "Aren't you that woman that was kidnapped?"

Less attention was given to the question of what happened to Joe Alexander and sons, the deprogrammers, or more to the point, what *should* happen to them.

To prosecute or not to prosecute? The question got tossed around like the hot potato it was.

At first, I felt my hands were tied, since I had made a verbal promise to my mother at the deprogramming house: "Don't worry, Mum, I won't press charges." I intended to keep the promise. Much as I resented my parents for what they'd done, I had no wish to send them to jail.

One day the Legal Department of our church called from New York City. This time, it was me they wanted to speak to. They wanted to congratulate me for surviving and escaping from my kidnappers.

"We're very grateful to you. We're very proud of you," said John, through the telephone. His voice was kind and the words were like a soothing balm to my soul. Then John wondered if I would please consider "going after" the deprogrammers, by pressing charges against them. It would mean a great deal to the Legal Department and might prevent future kidnappings, if we could get those felons put away. He was very persuasive. Not only that, the idea of having the deprogrammers put in jail was rather appealing to me. I felt they deserved it.

Sarah and I made an appointment with Detective Inspector Peter Robinson, who had saved me from the beach house. We told him I desired to "go after" the deprogrammers but that I wished to keep my promise to my mother as well.

"New Zealand *does* have an extradition treaty with the US. We could attempt to have the Alexanders extradited and tried here in New Zealand," said Robinson. "However, we can't selectively prosecute. If you want to prosecute them, you would have to prosecute everyone that was involved, including your own family members." I believed him. After all, he was my savior.

Therefore, it seemed, if I did the right thing and pressed charges against the deprogrammers, I would have to break my word to my mother. I then found myself in an awkward position, which, according to some, I should never have been put in at all.

Sarah and I had an appointment with Martin Knapp, the church's lawyer, at his office on the 6th floor of Landmark House on Queen Street. It was the first time I had met him. He was nice. His office was fancy. The furnishings looked expensive and there was a picture of Napoleon on the wall.

"I think the police are calling your bluff," said Knapp.

Peter Robinson was bluffing me? Immediately my opinion of Robinson sank to the plush carpet. Pam had already told me about Hugglestone. Were there no policemen who were trustworthy?

"They could have arrested all of those involved, while they were there at the house. There was nothing to stop them from doing that, nothing at all. If I compare your case to the 14-year-old in Oamaru who was abducted recently, I'm convinced that if the police had burst in on her and her captors, they'd have arrested them on the spot."

"But in my case, they didn't arrest anyone. They seem to be leaving it up to me." I was confused.

"Exactly, and I think that's a little unusual."

"Also, it's hardly fair to put all that on her after what she's just been through," said Sarah, quietly. I appreciated her sympathy.

But I still wanted to try and do the right thing.

"So, it is possible to prosecute selectively?" I asked Knapp.

"Yes. I've seen it done."

"And if we were to try that, what do you think are the chances of being successful?"

Knapp had been representing the church in various legal battles over many years. Perhaps in anticipation of such a question, he had, close at hand, several thick binders of court transcripts from a case in the 1970s.

"This is the Mary Smith case. She was a divorced woman who got involved with the Unification Church. When her ex-husband got wind of it, he sued for custody of their two young daughters. Mary fought to keep the children, and I represented her. The opposition to the church was extraordinary. They brought witness after witness who told all manner of horror stories." He opened one binder to show me a sample. I read something about Moonies begging on the streets, and Moonies in white vans with no windows, transporting young people around the countryside. It did sound scary.

"If you were to bring a case against your kidnappers, I would be happy to represent you. You would most probably be looking at a long, drawn-out, highly publicized trial. You need to know what you'd be up against, in terms of the attitude of judge and jury, which is heavily determined by popular opinion, unfortunately. I cannot say with confidence that such a case could be easily won."

"So, what happened with Mary Smith? Was she allowed to keep her children?"

"She was allowed to keep the children, on condition that she ceased to have any relationship with the Unification Church."

Sarah and I looked at each other. I'd never heard of Mary Smith, and imagined that I might never meet her, based on that unfortunate judgment.

"That is so unfair," I said.

"Yes," said Knapp. "It's also unfair that the deprogrammers were able to leave the country because the police didn't arrest them."

After that conversation with Mr. Knapp, we let go of the idea of prosecuting. We never spoke of it again. I felt bad because I had some idea of what was at stake. I felt like a coward. I hated to disappoint John and the others in the Legal Department. But what could I do?

Deprogramming, however, is unmistakably an example of the end justifying the means. Crimes (kidnapping and false imprisonment) are committed and then justified in order to rescue the brainwashed convert. I maintain that persons engaging in or condoning such criminal behavior have no solid platform on which to make their allegations against new religious movements. They must first renounce their own vigilante tactics.
—Lee Coleman, MD, Psychiatrist in Berkeley, California

34 - AFTERMATH

The public is generally unaware that this [deprogramming] is a crime whose perpetrators have victimized thousands of people of virtually every religious group in America. Ironically, the public believes that it is the religious groups that imprison members and hold them against their will. Further, the public believes that when deprogramming occurs, it is only in the context of cults, and thus is to be tolerated. The real story of this violent abuse of religious liberty is yet to be told.

—Dr Mose Durst, in *To Bigotry, No Sanction*

My parents loudly and publicly complained that I hadn't been home for seven years. That fact was true, yet the spin they put on it was entirely misleading. They blamed the Unification Church for my long absence. Ironically, I would have gladly attended Christmases and other important family gatherings, just as most of the other members did. I have a vivid memory of one December in Melbourne. Out of 20 or so members, only three of us were still in the center over Christmas, since everyone else had gone home to spend the holidays with their families. Carl, our English missionary, noticing how depressed and homesick I was, tried to cheer me up by taking the three of us out to see a Mad Max movie.

Hard as it was, I chose not to go home, for fear that I might run into a faith-breaking situation and as it turned out, my fear was well-founded. Yet my parents illogically continued to blame "the Moonies."

It was Sarah's idea for me to visit my family and try to patch things up. On some level, I knew it was the right thing to do, but another part of me wanted to cut off and never see or speak to them again. I was not mentally ready yet, for any "Kumbaya" experience, but agreed to it anyway, for the sake of peacemaking.

The best part was that Bob came from America to go with me on the visit. It was somewhat natural that my parents ought to meet their new son-in-law, and this seemed like an opportune time. Besides that, he would be a natural bodyguard. With him around it was unlikely they would try any monkey-business, like another kidnapping, so I would be safe. My barrel-chested Viking was a gentle soul who wouldn't hurt an ant, but he was also strong enough to defend himself or me if the need ever arose.

When Bob first arrived, I was as nervous as a schoolgirl with a crush. It was the evening of August 27 when he arrived in Auckland. Someone had gone to pick him up from the airport, and I was so anxious that I hadn't been able to eat dinner. I was in the prayer room, trying to calm myself, when suddenly he walked in and sat down on the floor with me. I didn't know what to say or how to act. His first words were not what I expected.

"I have a song I wrote for you...

True Parents are here

we can feel their love so clear

When we keep ourselves away from the other side..."

It was lovely and comforting and suddenly I was able to relax and regain my composure. Soon we were chatting like old friends.

Sarah urged us to have a legal wedding ceremony in preparation for our trip to see the relatives. If anything *did* happen to me, he would then be considered next of kin. On August 31, we were married at the Registrar's Office in downtown Auckland, with Sarah and Pam as our witnesses.

When we first arrived at the Registry and explained why we were there, the lady behind the counter was friendly and eager to help.

First, she would have to locate the appropriate paperwork. "Won't be a tick!"

"I hope not," said Bob, unfamiliar with the expression.

I remember laughing so hard with Pam and Sarah that we almost doubled over. That was another good thing about Bob—he made me laugh and it felt so good.

During the ceremony, the Registrar made us laugh as well, by accidentally saying, "Do you take this man to be your lawfully wedded wife?" Again, we all fell apart.

At the end, she asked Bob, "Would you like to kiss the bride?"

"No thanks, I'll wait." More uncontrollable laughter. It must have been one of the funniest weddings ever.

The following day, things got serious again. Bob and I took a plane to the South Island for our visit to the relatives. Now it was Bob's turn to be nervous. He was seeing his in-laws for the first time, and his were not just regular in-laws. It must have been extremely daunting to be the "church husband" of the cultist daughter of the now-famously hostile parents. The closer we got to Invercargill, the more he fidgeted. I felt bad for him but couldn't think of anything to say that might ease his anxiety. I wasn't exactly looking forward to the visit either.

My parents and some other family members met us at the airport. My brother Paul looked happy to see us. "You were really good on TV!" But other than that, the welcome was strained and awkward, which set the tone for the rest of our visit. Bob and I stayed close together, needing each other's support.

When we got to my parents' house, Mum looked at me with her frowny face. "Separate rooms or together?" I couldn't read the meaning behind her irritated expression. Was she annoyed that we might be in separate bedrooms, or was it distasteful that we might want to share a bed? I didn't care to know and didn't bother to ask.

"Separate." We were still in our betrothal period.

As we entered the dining room, someone turned on the radio.

"Korean Airline Flight 007 has been shot down over Soviet airspace. All 269 passengers and crew are believed to have died."

Bob and I looked at each other in shock. So many different thoughts rushed into my consciousness. The Cold War was heating up. Was this the beginning of a new era of death and destruction? Also, we'd just disembarked from a passenger airline. How safe was air travel anymore? In addition, our church was from Korea and we knew a lot of Koreans. Could any of our members have been on that flight?

"Wow," I said, hoping to start a conversation, but nobody else besides my "church husband" seemed particularly interested.

"You were angry on TV," said Mum, accusingly. In my family there were unwritten rules. Thou shalt not be angry. Thou shalt not be fat. Thou shalt not join strange new religions. I'd broken all of them.

I ignored the dig and sat down with Bob at the dining table near the radio, hoping to hear more news. The radio sat on a small bookcase, whose contents I examined out of curiosity. I felt a sinking feeling in my gut. Every book was a classic from my mother's anti-cult arsenal. Were they usually there, or had she placed them strategically for my homecoming? They sat in a neat pile, tormenting me: *The Moon is not the Son*, *Kingdom of the Cults*, *Snapping,* Ted Patrick's *Let Our Children Go!* and others. *Hate literature*. As I thumbed through some of the volumes, they seemed to radiate fear and confusion; and as I placed them back on the shelf, my hands were trembling.

Being in my parents' home again after a long absence also brought back pleasant memories. Growing up in Invercargill, I had a large extended family. One aunt had let me borrow every delightfully musty volume of her *Anne of Green Gables* series as well as all the rest of her Lucy Maud Montgomery collection. Another gave me a manicure set when I was confirmed; I could still remember the pretty pale blue pouch, with silhouettes of tiny blue cherubs on a circle of white. Uncle Ted said my hands looked graceful when I played piano. I remembered Christmases, christenings and First Communions with hordes of relatives and home-baked treats, the solidness of family connections stretching around me like a warm blanket.

But going home that September of 1983, the blanket was gone and instead there was a wall. The barrier which had grown up between my mother and me had extended and thickened enough to separate me from my entire clan. It was a wall of lies, fears and misunderstandings which I felt powerless to overcome. I hoped I might find a crack in it, a point of weakness where someone might reach across and show regret or remorse for what had happened. I hoped for even one person who might offer sympathy or empathy.

But no, all the sympathy was devoted to my mother. "Poor Mary," I could read it in their eyes. "Poor Mary, she spent all that money and her daughter's still in the Moonies, and she's not even grateful." They were full of admiration for her bravery and resourcefulness. "Mary was amazing," wrote an uncle in a card. I was jealous. I wanted them to admire me, not her.

Relatives came to dinner with faces so grim you would think someone had died. It was a solid wall, not a crack in sight.

"It wasn't *that* bad, was it?" said my sister Anne, referring to the deprogramming. I looked into her big blue eyes and knew she'd already made up her mind.

"You weren't there," I shot back.

Auntie Mary-Ray came over for afternoon tea and polite conversation. On her way out, she looked at me through narrowed eyes and proclaimed, "I hope all your mother's dreams come true!" before sailing off through the ranch slider door. Bob held my hand and squeezed it.

It would have been much harder being back in my parents' home and my parents' world, without Bob. Having him there meant I had at least one friend on my side of the wall. The funny thing about Bob being there was that the relatives barely seemed to notice him.

Neighbors were different. One day in Invercargill we visited my old neighbors, the Killeens, a tall broad-shouldered Irishman and his wife, who had been good friends of my grandparents. As we entered their small house, Jim Killeen looked at Bob and boomed, "You got a nice man!"

That was when I realized no one else ever said anything like that. Except for my favorite cousin Kathleen, who found his American accent extremely sexy, no one acknowledged my marriage and my husband. No one asked Bob anything about his family, birthplace, hobbies, hopes, dreams or any of the normal things you ask the new husband of your close relative. No one said "Congratulations" or asked about our future. I guessed they saw him as not a real husband, just a "church husband" as the newspapers had said.

Auntie Mary-Pat lived on a sheep farm about 60 miles from my parents' house, with my uncle and their five children. One weekend, Mum called her on the phone.

"Hello, Mary-Pat? This is Mary-Paul. I'm wondering if I could bring my daughter and her husband for a visit." Mary-Pat said she'd be delighted.

For our visit she cooked a huge Sunday roast, in the tradition of astonishing hospitality that farming families in Southland are known for. We sat around the room, our plates piled high with food. Every so often she would come by me and Bob with loaded serving dishes in hand. "Have some more ham, or lamb, or mashed potatoes! How about some gravy?" The look on her face said here, have some more love and kindness, you probably need it, you poor dears!

The woman was known for her natural goodness and generosity, and Uncle Pat had been fortunate to find such a wife as he approached middle age. She not only knew how to be a farmer's wife but had given him a houseful of beautiful children as well.

I wondered how Mary-Pat would have reacted if one her kids joined a new religion. I imagined her visiting the "cult" and coming away saying what lovely people they were. Different, but nice, and who are we to judge, she might say in that gentle voice of hers.

I envied my cousins. I wished my mother was more like Mary-Pat.

My Mum had built a dam around the large reservoir of her heart. She could completely withhold the flow of love at will or allow carefully controlled releases when appropriate. Mary-Pat's heart was free like a waterfall, able to flow over jagged rocks, walls and all manner of obstacles.

I knew which one I wanted to emulate. But I would have to fight a natural tendency to resemble the woman who had raised me and given me birth.

***

—Public Opinion Page, Southland Times, August 19, 1983

Sir,

So the Unification Church or Moonies want the deprogrammers barred from entering New Zealand. Surely that is an admission of the methods they use to get young unsuspecting people into their cult, for that is what it is.

I hope the Christian people of this province thank Mary and Paul Ryan for bringing out in the open their heartbreak over Maree. At least it may put on guard other young people, especially those travelling overseas, but they are also here in New Zealand. Remember it might be your son or daughter or grandson or granddaughter they claim next

And to those people who give donations or buy buttonholes or such like items, without making very sure of what it is for, do not be taken in by them saying it is to be used to help young people of New Zealand. It is more likely to be used to make Mr. Moon and his organization even more wealthy.

Most of all let us remember Maree and her family in our prayers and let them know that there are a lot of people who are thinking of them and praying for them and others in similar circumstances that one day they will have the joy of a united family.

Maree's Aunt
Invercargill

35 - "BLOODY MOONIES!"

We must always take sides. Neutrality helps the oppressor, never the victim. Silence encourages the tormentor, never the tormented.
—Elie Wiesel

Some months later…

A pro-Nicaragua rally was set to take place, organized by the New Zealand Labor Party's Nicaraguan Support Committee. In the thick of the Cold War, the Unification Church was fiercely anti-Communist long before anti-Communism was stylish.

"Counter-protest! Let's go!" Peter was always ready for some action. "How about it, Mark?"

Mark, a burly former rugby player, might come in handy if things got physical.

The strategy was to try to upstage or simply stir up trouble at pro-Communist events by showing up and presenting a different viewpoint. In the case of Nicaragua, they could protest that the new Sandinista government was engaged in an attempted genocide of the Miskito Indians. They painted slogans accordingly:

Marxism, Leninism, Murderism.

Sandinistas are murderers!

Stop the Miskito genocide!

Off they went, a small band of brothers armed with poster-board signs, acting on behalf of concerned citizens rather than officially representing the church. I might have joined them, but Sarah cautioned against it since my face might still be recognized.

They quietly mingled into the noisy crowd that had gathered on Queen Street, holding their signs higher as they went deeper into the heart of the group.

One of the first to spot the counter-protest was the colorful Mayor of Waitemata, Tim Shadbolt, a veteran of protest movements since the Vietnam era and author of the controversial memoir, *Bullshit and Jellybeans.*

"You guys don't belong here!" he yelled, dropping his own sign and taking hold of Peter's.

"Hey, leave my sign alone." Peter gripped it more tightly.

There was pushing, shoving and a tug-of-war, during which Peter's sign started to rip. To save expenses, the brothers had re-used the backs of old signs and stapled them together.

Tim in his leftist tantrum was tearing the sign further, which caused the staples to come undone. In doing so, he was able to read what was underneath.

"*Free Maree!?* Free Maree! Hah! You're the Moonies! The bloody Moonies!" Shadbolt gloated at the unexpected exposure.

Busted!

Their cover blown, the brothers made a hasty retreat from the scene.

Fifteen years later, having lost his seat in Waitemata, Shadbolt resurfaced in my hometown, Invercargill, where he became the longest-standing mayor in the history of New Zealand.

I don't care where, as long as I'm mayor.
—Tim Shadbolt, referencing his dual mayoralties

EPILOGUE

And those who would see wonderful things
must often be ready to travel alone.
—Unknown

People often ask me how my relationship with my parents is now, after all that happened, and whether I've forgiven them. Relationship-wise, my father died in 1996 of lung cancer and at the time of writing, my mother is in the advanced stages of frail dementia; so, there is no real relationship to speak of.

I had hoped that in her condition, my mother would achieve a loss of her hostility toward my new religion along with her loss of memories. That was not the case. In 2012, a relative told my mother that Reverend Moon, founder of the Unification Church, had passed on.

"I'm glad he's dead!" she said.

I was crushed when I heard her response. My mother was still immersed in her sea of bitterness.

Concerning forgiveness, had I been completely unforgiving, I could have given full vent to the rage I felt in 1983 by doing two things: first, pressing charges against all my kidnappers in the hope that they would experience the full extent of punishment under the law; and second, cutting off from my parents forever. I did neither of those things. Instead I began trying to rebuild the relationship little by little, to the best of my ability. Any residual ill feeling I experience is due to lack of closure, rather than lack of forgiveness.

I had hoped that someday, my parents might validate me and the choices I made, and that they might even be proud of me. After all, I had a good life with my Viking husband, Bob. We eventually moved in together, consummating our marriage with a holy honeymoon ceremony, during which we accomplished the requisite positions I had been so curious about. Bob proved to be an enthusiastic lover who helped me overcome my maidenly reticence. As a result, we enjoyed a fulfilling marriage which produced four outstanding and adventurous children. In 1992 we settled in Yuba County, Northern California, close to where Bob grew up. With my husband's support and encouragement, I built a successful piano teaching business, and also became known for various kinds of community activism. I believe I became a better person by knowing Reverend Moon.

When my father was on his deathbed in 1996, I was able to visit him and ask for his forgiveness for all the trouble I'd caused him. "We all have to forgive," was the response. I hoped for more. I hoped he might apologize and ask *my* forgiveness for the trouble he'd caused me, but that didn't happen. Because of that, even though I wanted to, I never spoke the words, "I forgive you," before he breathed his last.

My dad's final illness and consequent death were a tense and difficult time. Mum, in her grief, was apparently looking for someone to blame for the untimely loss of her beloved husband at the relatively young age of 70. They'd been married 41 years. "Anger causes cancer," she proclaimed, glaring pointedly in my direction. Her look meant clearly that Dad's death was all my fault, and that if I hadn't made him so angry, he might still be alive. Never mind that he smoked "cancer sticks" for forty years.

Months later, while sorting through Dad's belongings, Mum discovered, carefully stored in one of his file boxes, a poem written in a calligraphic hand. Since the mysterious poem was titled, "*forgive me, moon-child,*" Mum sent it to me. Although the script was unfamiliar and the writer unknown, the poem helped me make peace with my father. It was as if he were calling out for forgiveness from beyond the grave.

It turns out that my father, who rarely picked up hitchhikers, once gave a ride to a local poet by the name of Michael O'Leary. During their journey together, my father talked while Michael listened. Family members have speculated that this conversation gave birth to the poem. Others insist that it was not O'Leary, but another hitch-hiking poet, Geoff Soper, who wrote it. Will the real *moon-child* author please stand up?

Mum and I maintained a basic, though restrained, mother-daughter relationship. She helped us with the down payment for our first home, sent Christmas and birthday packages and was attentive to her grandchildren.

I recall the last visit we ever had, before my father became ill. It was relatively pleasant. My parents came to see us in California, on their way to Ireland. Dad had made a wooden Celtic cross which he would present as a gift to some Irish relatives. At the time, we had three small children and were living in a two-bedroom apartment. Bob borrowed a friend's RV and parked it next to our building for my parents to stay in. One day, I was serving lunch to my parents in our small kitchen, while Dad bounced our youngest child, and first son, on his lap. The beautiful, happy baby had his granddad's brown eyes and black hair. Mum complimented me on the corn-bread I'd made and even asked for the recipe.

But some attitudes never change. Trying to make conversation, I mentioned to Mum that sometimes, people say I look like the actress, Meryl Streep. I hoped she might agree, but instead, I got a frowny face and total lack of comprehension of the comparison.

"But she's *thin*!" said Mum.

Incidentally, while living in Northern California, I got to meet the mysterious Kristina, alleged inventor of mind control techniques for the Oakland church, as well as Dr and Mrs. Durst, about whom I'd heard so many outlandish things from Joe Alexander, Jr.

Just as I suspected, they were outstanding people of moral excellence, who I hope and imagine will be counted among the great saints of these troubled times.

***

"forgive me, moon-child"

remember I'm an old man & rigid
but I love you
please forgive me for my intolerance
a structure I've learnt which guides me
because its true, I'm blind to other possibilities
I love you
please forgive me for my intolerance

please visit with your family & supporting friends
tons of room & welcome
please be gentle on us & our beliefs
we are not very able & need to cling to them
or we will be lost
just as you need to be a follower of the Rev. Moon
& would be threatened by ridicule & disbelief

the common ground between us
is our genes
& the flow of love easy & strong
much shared
let's work on our differences & look for our beauty
& our wisdom, our tolerance
I love you, please forgive me my intolerance

17 - 10 - 88

The End

Cast of Main Characters

Faith-Breaking Team
Joe Alexander Sr
Joe Alexander Jr
Jerry Alexander (night guard & gofer)
Mary Harvey (guard)
Rosalind Menzies
John Fileul (night guard)
Pat Ryan (Maree's brother, night guard)
Bridget Gardner
Geraldine (observer)
Mrs. Mary Ryan (cook)

Rescue Team
Sarah*, UC National Leader
Chris Newman, UC Public Affairs Officer
Geoff Prentice, Public Affairs Assistant
Pam, Church Secretary & Bookkeeper
Margaret*, center member
Grant, center member
Peter Holdem, center member and seasonal fisherman
Mark Cleaver, center member, fisherman and former rugby player
Warren, home member and employee of Air New Zealand
Martin Knapp, partner at legal firm, Johnston, Prichard & Fee
David Meek, former UC member
Tai, Private Investigator
Mike Ferris, Scientologist and friend of Chris

Police
Detective Inspectors Gerry Hugglestone & Peter Robinson
*not their actual names

AFTERWORD

As many of you know, the Unification Church of Japan has suffered for years from the scourge of "deprogramming" ...Japanese UC members still live in fear that any visit home for a family reunion or birthday celebration will turn into their worst nightmare.

—Ichiko Sudo, Program Director, Religious Liberty and Human Rights Committee, February 8, 2010

"Bob, your wife's been kidnapped."

I'll never forget those shocking words spoken to me on a muggy August evening outside Chicago in 1983.

It was a tough month. My mother was on her death bed in Marysville, California, and I didn't know where my wife, Maree, was.

I first met Maree in the Grand Ballroom of the New Yorker Hotel in Manhattan in June of 1982, when we were introduced by Reverend Sun Myung Moon. Less than a week after our matching, we were blessed in marriage on July 1 in a record-breaking 2,075 couple mass wedding ceremony at Madison Square Garden.

Before moving in together we had a long-distance relationship and grew to know each other better through letters and occasional phone calls. Although we were in different hemispheres, our fondness for each other slowly developed. When I learned of Maree's kidnapping, I felt powerless. What could I do to help her while I was in the United States and she was held captive in New Zealand? All I could do was pray for her release. Ten days after her abduction, my prayers were answered. She was rescued from her captors. That same day, my mother died.

On July 1, 2018, Maree and I celebrated our thirty-sixth wedding anniversary.

I joined the Unification Church (UC) in 1978. Throughout the years, multitudes of members left the church for a host of reasons: some couldn't handle the persecution or period of celibacy. Others weren't happy with their suggested spouse. Or didn't like Reverend Moon's politics or theology. Or were disillusioned because there were prostitutes in Korea. The reasons for leaving were endless. One church friend left because her parents offered to buy her a new car. Most of those people left on their own volition and didn't need helicopter parents on steroids kidnapping them and imposing their will upon them.

Of course, members who were kidnapped, "deprogrammed," lost their faith and caved into their parents' control, might say such things as, "I'm so glad they saved me. If it wasn't for them, I'd still be peddling posies on street corners and raising my arms shouting *Mansei* at Moonie gatherings."

What else are they going to say? "Well, although people around me were leaving on their own, I was too spineless to do that. I'm so glad Mommy and Daddy were there to rescue me."

Their response might be, "But, but I couldn't leave. I was under mind-control!" (which didn't work for Patty Hearst).

Earnest Hemingway said, "Writing isn't all that difficult. All you have to do is stare at the typewriter until you bleed". Likewise, our writers' group encouraged Maree to "open a vein" when sharing her story.

Often, as she read me drafts for *Free Maree*, I could sense her angst as she revisited the betrayal of friends, family and the indifference of police.

When she wrote the chapter "Aftermath", she shared how incredibly lonely it was for her during the many Christmases when most of the UC members were spending time with their families.

"I was too afraid of what my parents might do if I went home. Other parents weren't like them. Why did mine have to be so closed-minded?"

Fortunately, fines and imprisonment have, for the most part, eliminated the medieval-like practice of deprogramming in most democratic countries. However, it still may exist in Japan. Hopefully, the convictions of deprogrammer Takeshi Miyamura and Christian pastor Satoshi Moriyama in 2011, for their culpability in the confinement of UC member, Toru Goto, *for over twelve years*, will finally put a stop to forced faith breaking.

My grandfather offered to pay to have me kidnapped and deprogrammed away from the "Moonist Cult" but my parents weren't interested. They trusted me to make my own decisions.

Although it was often parents who hated the church and had their adult children kidnapped that made the headlines, many parents were quite happy their children joined the church. For example, one friend told me his dad wrote Reverend Moon a letter and thanked him for saving his son's life. That same friend designed his house, so that his elderly mother-in-law could spend her final months in relative comfort before her passing. Many UC members have provided similar helpful kindnesses.

I'm so proud of Maree for writing this book. I've witnessed how hard she's worked researching, conducting interviews, and as she says, "rewriting the rewrites of the rewrites."

In addition to her writing, Maree has built a successful piano-teaching business, and provides scholarships to many of her students, plus she volunteers for Toastmasters, Lions Club, Women's Federation for World Peace (WFWP) and recently chaired the local Tri-Counties Music Competition. As a music professional, she has been the church organist for our local Episcopal Church, as well as Mt. Olivet Baptist Church, the Beale Air Force Base Chapel and others.

While attending a WFWP retreat in Atlanta, Maree was inspired by the work of a fellow WFWP member who organizes an annual festival in honor of Reverend Dr. Martin Luther King Jr.

Eventually, she arranged a local interchurch musical event for MLK weekend, hosted by the Mormon church, which included a sermon by the fiery African-American preacher Dr. Carl Dorn from Mt. Olivet Baptist Church.

A year later, Mt. Olivet reciprocated as host church. While addressing the standing-room-only gathering, Pastor Dorn looked over to Maree, smiled, and said, "Sister Maree, you have a special spirit about you."

Years later, she gave a two-minute speech, on the need for repentance, to people gathered for a Martin Luther King service at the African Methodist Episcopal Church in Marysville, my hometown. She ended by reading a prayer of repentance by the Rev. Sun Myung Moon, which brought tears to my eyes and to many others.

Maree, you indeed have a special spirit about you.

Bob Gauper – AKA "Church Husband"

ACKNOWLEDGEMENTS

First, I thank my dear husband, Bob, who got me started on this project and without whom this book baby would never even have been conceived. Not only has he been my chief cheer-leader throughout the long process, he also undertook and completed the gargantuan task of self-publishing. I'm in awe of his intelligence, resourcefulness and determination.

Looking back, I remember Susan Luccini and her memoir class at Amicus Books in Marysville, who coached and gave encouragement in the early days of gestation; also, the brilliant James and Kara Davis who owned Amicus Books. We miss it, and them.

When confidence waned, and termination seemed inevitable, the irrepressible Larry Moffitt gave an empowering webinar on memoir writing and some personal mentoring which got me back on track, with a vengeance. Larry, you're my hero!

Miraculously, while trying to organize a meet-up, Bob discovered that some serious writers were already meeting in Marysville. We started to attend the twice-monthly meetings which are facilitated by the kind and talented Dr. Susan McNally. This amazing group graciously guided me through the completion of my memoir with generous helpings of their time, energy, and moral support. If Dr. McNally was the wise midwife of my book baby, Roger Funston, Diane Funston and Minerva Rebecca Davis were her faithful support team.

I thank Larry, Jennifer, Susan, Louise, Chuck, Lesley, Cory, Nanci, Chris, Mary, Warren, Randall, Bento, and all my Beta Readers, who gave needed validations and excellent suggestions for improvement.

I also acknowledge ongoing conversations with key characters Chris Newman, Martin Knapp, Warren, Peter, Pam, and others, who helped fill in the gaps. I could not have finished my story without them.

Bob and I wish to appreciate Bento Leal for his helpful advice on publishing and marketing.

Researching news articles from the 80's was a challenge. I had hoped to find them through the Internet, but most online archives don't go back that far. You have to search in local libraries for a particular publication's history, a challenging task for someone living on the other side of the world. Fortunately, our good friends, Warren, Barbara, and Unhee, were willing and able to find four *New Zealand Herald* articles, nine *Auckland Star* articles and an in-depth feature from *The New Zealand Listener*. Warren also found Myna Bird cartoons I requested. I am indebted to them for their diligence.

Also, many thanks to the very helpful woman at the Auckland Central Library and Research Center, and staff at the Invercargill Public Library.

Finally, a shout-out to Mark Hanlon and all the Facebook friends who helped tweak our cover design with their input. You guys are awesome, a virtual village of cheerleaders.

And even if it sounds corny, it *does* take a village to birth a book baby.

APPENDIX 1 "CONTRA PESTIFERAM DOCTRINAM"

Everyone has the right to freedom of thought, conscience and religion; this right includes freedom to change his religion or belief.
—Article 18 - United Nations - Universal Declaration of Human Rights

The tribulations suffered by Thomas Aquinas and Francis of Assisi are among the more noteworthy historical precedents to the modern phenomenon of deprogramming.

In the 15th century, the Spanish Inquisition used torture and death threats to influence heretics to return to the Catholic Church.

In the 1970s, deprogrammers employed a range of physical and psychological abuses designed to coerce a victim to renounce his or her faith.

Behavioral scientists have called deprogramming "the new exorcism," based on its similar methodology.

Legal scholar Dean M. Kelley called it "protracted spiritual gang-rape."

Lawyer John LeMoult compared the power of deprogrammers to that of Nazis over their prisoners.

Ted Patrick, known as "Black Lightning", is considered the father of deprogramming in America. Patrick embarked on a brazen crusade against new religious movements after his son spent a total of four hours with the "Children of God" in 1971. Despite his lack of education beyond the 10th Grade, Patrick set himself up as an expert on "the cults", and was willing to go to any lengths, legal or otherwise, to remove people from them.

Not only religious converts were targeted. According to Wikipedia, in 1980 Susan Wirth, a 35-year-old teacher living in San Francisco, was abducted by her parents to be deprogrammed from her leftist political leanings. Patrick was paid $27,000 for the deprogramming attempt, in which Wirth was handcuffed to a bed for two weeks and denied food. She was held for thirty-one days.

In 1981 Patrick was fined for the kidnapping of 19-year-old Stephanie Riethmiller of Ohio, who was taken to Alabama by deprogrammers because her parents objected to her alleged lesbian relationship with a roommate. Riethmiller was held against her will and repeatedly raped. Later she unsuccessfully filed charges against all the people involved.

Patrick's highly publicized activities spawned an industry of sorts and as a result, thousands of deprogrammings were carried out in America and beyond.

A leading anti-cult group, the "Cult Awareness Network" (CAN) was regularly a co-conspirator, providing a liaison between parents of "cult" members and the deprogramming networks.

Among the deprogrammers influenced by Patrick were Joe Alexander, a former used-car salesman from Ohio who apprenticed himself to Patrick for a year before taking off on his own. His son, Joe Alexander Jr., also became a nationally known deprogrammer. The Alexanders once claimed to have conducted at least 600 deprogrammings.

Convicted jewel thief Rick Ross, American "cult" specialist and director of the Cult Education Institute, claims to have been involved in more than 500 deprogramming cases in various countries.

When Ted Patrick first started his crusade, he was frequently able to convince the courts and law enforcement that his illegal actions were justified because they represented the lesser of two evils. But by the 1980s the tables were turning; the courts had started to crack down and take a much dimmer view of deprogramming.

In 1980 Patrick was sentenced to one year in prison and fined $5,000 for abducting and attempting to deprogram 26-year old Roberta McElfish, a waitress from Tucson, Arizona. He was convicted of conspiracy, kidnapping and false imprisonment.

By 1982 Joe Alexander Jr had also run into problems. He was convicted of kidnapping and received a two-year deferred sentence, on condition that he discontinue his illegal activities.

* * *

In 1981, Michael Treacy, an Australian Unification Church member, was kidnapped in Canberra and taken to Bateman's Bay for a deprogramming session under the supervision of Americans Erica Heftman and William Knapp. Three other men assisted in the deprogramming: an ex-policeman, a long-distance runner and an ex-member of the Unification Church who had joined briefly in California.

After three days of confinement Michael had a prepared breakdown during which he pretended to renounce his faith. He was then taken to a farm north of Sydney near Gosford. After another 6 days, when the deprogrammers had car trouble, Mike offered to check out their engine. Thinking he'd fixed the problem he recommended a test drive, to which they agreed. Michael test drove the car 62 miles to Sydney's Central Police Station, where he promptly filed a report.

Fortunately, there was an abundance of deprogramming literature inside the vehicle which he was able to present as evidence.

Michael then attempted to prosecute the whole gang for kidnapping and false imprisonment. The deprogrammers were charged, and his parents were implicated as well. A prima facie case was established which meant the case would go to trial.

After 6 months the Queen's Counsel (respected lawyer) for the deprogrammers died suddenly and six months later, Mike's father died suddenly too. The Attorney General for New South Wales decided, under the circumstances, that the trial should be discontinued. The deprogrammers (Heftman and Knapp) were then allowed to return to the U.S., "much depleted of funds, as they couldn't work in Australia", according to Treacy.

* * *

Thomas Aquinas, having resisted his parents' attempts to forcibly remove him from the Dominicans, went on to become a priest, philosopher, and theologian who ultimately achieved sainthood. The same Saint Thomas wrote what was possibly the first official denunciation of deprogramming in his essay, "Contra pestiferam doctrinam retrahentiam homines a religionis ingress", which translates as:

"Against the Pernicious Teaching of Those Dragging Youth Away from Entering the Religious life."

APPENDIX 2
TORU GOTO

In February 2008, a penniless and emaciated Mr. Toru Goto of Tokyo was expelled from an apartment after spending over twelve years in confinement in apartment prisons throughout Japan. During his incarceration, family members mentally and physically abused him and hired professional deprogrammers to force Goto to change his Unification Church beliefs.

While wandering the streets of Tokyo, Goto recounted, "Although I was free, I was physically debilitated…I was attacked by a feeling of anxiety as to how I would survive the situation."

After police refused to help, Goto continued along the streets of Tokyo and had to use both hands to support his knees in order to walk. After "walking" for around four hours he lacked the strength to cross an intersection and remembered, "It was already night…It was the coldest month of the year. I realized I might die that night. I could be frozen to death. I mentally prepared myself for martyrdom."

However, he determined to go forward, "even if I had to crawl," and miraculously ran into a Unification Church sister who paid a taxi to bring him to the church center.

"I had not been treated as a human being during the 12-year confinement. I was so touched by her warm heart that I had not felt for so many years that I couldn't stop tears running down."

After going to the church center, he was served dinner and then brought to Isshin Hospital and admitted for 42 days and treated for muscular atrophy, anemia and malnutrition.

After his recuperation, Goto sued his captors and was awarded an equivalent of $47,000 U.S. from his brother, sister, sister-in-law, deprogrammer Takashi Miyamura and Pastor Yasutomo Matsunaga of the Niitsu Evangelical Church.

Freedom Rights Project co-founder Aaron Rhodes, called the reward "paltry."

Pictures and more about Goto's story can be found at freemaree.com

ABOUT THE AUTHOR

I am an artist on a mission. I like to write about matters of the heart and things that are personal and important to me. One of those things is religious freedom. I believe that adult children must be allowed to live their lives according to their own consciousness.

Deprogramming is an extreme expression of intolerance. It is abusive. It is a violation of personal freedoms. Organizations and individuals such as the police, established churches, mental health professionals, and media giants like TED, all of whom have openly supported deprogramming are guilty of enabling and perpetuating this heinous crime. They must be held accountable.

I am a mother of four extraordinarily gifted adult children who are perfectly free to make their own choices in life. I am a piano teacher and church organist. I am a peace activist who dreams of the world someday becoming a peaceful global village as taught by the Reverend Sun Myung Moon and his wife Hak Ja Han Moon.

B.A, English, Otago University, New Zealand
Associate of Trinity College, London (ATCL)

Thank you for purchasing and reading *FREE MAREE.* I hope you found it informative and entertaining. If you'd like to find out more about my work, please visit my website. Also, a sincere review, good or bad, on Amazon and/or social media would be most appreciated.

65224329R00149

Made in the USA
Middletown, DE
02 September 2019